Risk and

Designed and written by Barry J. McLoughlin.

Copyright © 1996 McLoughlin MultiMedia Publishing Ltd. All rights reserved. ISBN Number: 1-886712-03-4

This material is protected by copyright and other proprietary rights and may not be reproduced in any form whatsoever, without prior written permission except in the case of brief quotations embodied in critical articles and reviews.

For information write to Barry McLoughlin Associates Inc.
In Washington:
1825 Eye Street NW, Suite 400, Washington, D.C. 20006.
In Canada:
55 Metcalfe Street, Suite 1030, Ottawa, Ontario K1P 6L5.
Internet address: www.mclomedia.com
Email: communicate@mclomedia.com
To place an order please see the Appendix Tab at the end of this booklet.

Published by: McLoughlin MultiMedia Publishing Ltd., a subsidiary of Barry McLoughlin Associates Inc.

Washington, D.C.	Princeton, N.J.	Ottawa, Canada
202-429-5243	609-951-2204	613-230-9235
Fax: 202-429-9574	Fax: 609-520-1702	Fax: 613-230-2630

In North America call toll free: 1-800-663-3899

© 1996 McLoughlin MultiMedia Publishing Ltd.

Table of Contents

Introduction

- Foreword 1
- About the Company 2
- Introduction 4
- Risk 5
- Incident, Emergency and Crisis Framework 7
- Daily Incident 8
- Emergency 9
- Crisis 10

Risk

- Public Perception of Risk 15
- Factors Effecting Acceptability 15
- What to Watch Out For 16
- Three Guiding Principles 18
- Risk Management Decision Process 22
- Goals of Risk Communications Program 23
- Risk Communications Critical Path 38
- Verbals, Para-Verbals and Non-Verbals 40
- Communicating During a Public Meeting 41
- Quick Tips for Risk Communications 44
- Communicate With Power Risk Communications Planner™ 45

Public Consultations

- Why Consult 47
- 10 Keys to Developing a Consultation Process 50
- When to Hold Consultations 52
- Consultation Models 54
- Communicate with Power Information Loop™ 61

Emergency

- Emergency Response 63
- The Role of Initial Responders 67
- Internal Briefings 70

© 1996 McLoughlin MultiMedia Publishing Ltd.

Table of Contents

Crisis
- The Communicator's Responsibilities 73
- 6 Crisis Concepts 74
- 10 Principles of Effective Crisis Communications 77
- Crisis Communications Plan 80

Media Relations
- Overall Media Relations 95
- Risk Consultations and the Media 107
- Communicate With Power Risk Consultation Modeller™ 113
- Crises and the Media 116
- Initial Responders and the Media 118
- Develop a Media Strategy 120
- Media Center 134

Planning Tools
- Consultation is Key to Credibility 137
- Risk Management Decision Process 138
- Goals of a Risk Communications Strategy 139
- Communicate With Power:
  - Message Developer™ 140
  - Communications Planner™ 141
  - Public Consultations Decision-Maker™ 142
  - Consultation Loop™ 143
- Crisis Communications Plan 144
- Crisis Communications Team 146
- Communicate With Power Consultation Modeller™ 147
- Encountering the Media Issues Planner™ 148

Appendix
- Communicate With Power™ Tools and Seminars 149
- Order Form 153

© 1996 McLoughlin MultiMedia Publishing Ltd.

© 1996 *McLoughlin MultiMedia Publishing Ltd.*

Introduction

Foreword

Welcome to the first edition of the Communicate With Power® *Risk and Crisis Communications* Pocket Tips Booklet which marks the launch of the Communicate with Power® Gold Box set of pocket tips booklets. This booklet has been developed as a result of twelve years of crisis communications training as well as counseling public and private sector clients on the handling of risk issues.

This book is dedicated to my children, Caroline, Brendan and Liam - and all children - who are growing up in a high-risk world. McLoughlin MultiMedia Publishing Ltd. will donate 50¢ from each Risk and Crisis Communications booklet sold for programs to help children at risk.

Special thanks are due to Patricia Jenkins and Maureen Whitehead for help making this project a reality.

To Laura - my wife and partner who has helped me through many high-risk situations and a few crises thrown in for good measure - my love and gratitude.

Barry McLoughlin
May, 1996

McLoughlin MultiMedia Publishing Ltd.
The Principals

Barry J. McLoughlin, president, founded Barry McLoughlin Associates Inc. in 1984, following a television career as a writer, interviewer and producer. In demand as a conference speaker and media commentator, Barry designs the training programs and is author of the books and multimedia tools.
 Barry received his Master in Public Administration from Harvard University (1983).

Laura M. Peck, vice-president of Barry McLoughlin Associates Inc. since 1984, is a former broadcaster and teacher. A graduate of Dalhousie University (Bachelor of Arts 1977, Bachelor of Education 1978), Laura is responsible for conducting and coordinating seminars and media coaching sessions. She has coached political candidates and Fortune 500 CEOs in media and presentation skills.

Barry McLoughlin Associates Inc.

Barry McLoughlin Associates Inc. has developed an international reputation for quality communications skills training programs. The firm has assembled a team of seminar leaders, trained in the copyrighted communications techniques of the company. Barry McLoughlin Associates Inc. conducts seminars for major corporations, government agencies, national associations and labor unions throughout North America and through licensed distributors around the world.

All of the seminars are customized, skills-oriented, training programs conducted on an in-house, small group basis.

McLoughlin MultiMedia Publishing Ltd.

McLoughlin MultiMedia Publishing Ltd. is a subsidiary of Barry McLoughlin Associates Inc., and produces state-of-the-art communications tools.

The product line includes the 1996 I.A.B.C. Excel award-winning Encountering the Media ToolKit® as well as other software programs, booklets, videos and instructor kits in the copyrighted Communicate With Power® series of programs.

For more information on products and seminars, please turn to the Appendix.

Introduction

Comparatively few people will ever be directly involved in emergencies or crises. Even the handling of risk issues - those that affect public health, safety, the environment or financial security - will rarely directly engage massive numbers of the public. The vast majority of the public will judge an organization's response to the risk, emergency or crisis almost purely on the basis of media stories. Thus, the public's perception of the organization's response or actions will be mostly determined by the communications response.

Crises are not always negative experiences. The Chinese word for crisis is composed of two characters - one meaning danger, and the other opportunity.

It is easy to confuse the terms used to describe issues, incidents and events which require a communications response. The following pages attempt to clarify these terms.

© 1996 *McLoughlin MultiMedia Publishing Ltd.*

Risk Definitions

Traditionally, the expert's definition of risk has been, as follows:

$$\boxed{\text{The Amount of Hazard}} \times \boxed{\text{The Likelihood of Occurrence}} = \boxed{\text{RISK}}$$

It is a very technical definition but it doesn't do justice to the reality of communications. Dr. Peter Sandman, the director of the environmental communication research program and professor of journalism at Rutgers University is an acknowledged expert in risk communications. Dr. Sandman introduced into the equation the concept of Outrage*:

$$\boxed{\textbf{Hazard}} + \boxed{\textbf{Outrage}} = \boxed{\textbf{RISK}}$$

If the risk communications process doesn't anticipate and confront the issue of outrage then it will be difficult to manage it successfully.

---

* *Responding to Community Outrage, Sandman, Peter M., American Industrial Hygiene, Fairfax, VA, 1993.*

Risk Issue

An issue which poses potential hazard to the public, employees, shareholders or others who have a stake in the issue. These issues include threats to life, health, safety, the environment or financial security.

Risk Management

The systematic identification and analysis of risks and ways to control them which includes communicating with interested parties and analyzing, selecting and implementing control options.

Risk Communications

The risk communications framework is a continuum which supports, and operates throughout, the risk management process. It includes such activities as issue identification, stakeholder analysis, development of consultation and communication strategies, message development, working with the media, interactions with stakeholders, monitoring and evaluating the public dialogue.

Incident, Emergency and Crisis Framework

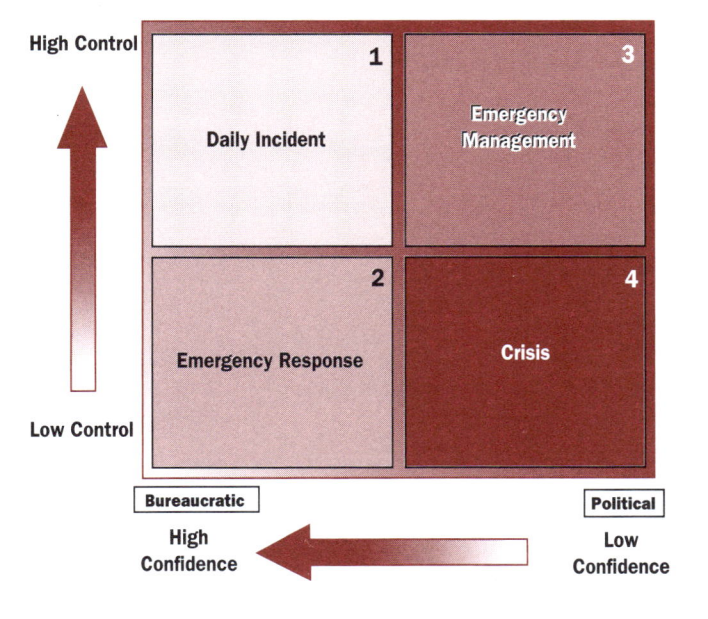

	High Control	
	1 Daily Incident	**3** Emergency Management
	2 Emergency Response	**4** Crisis
	Low Control	
	Bureaucratic / High Confidence	Political / Low Confidence

Source: Dr. Peter Meyboom, noted crisis management expert and C.A.O., City of Ottawa, Ontario, Canada.

Daily Incident (Quadrant 1)

A relatively minor occurrence, event or daily panic that may precipitate a public crisis.

For example, a fire, shooting, a lay-off notice, a dip in stock price. These kinds of incidents are common and, although they require resources to respond, they are manageable. Normal business can still take place while the incident is being handled. Control and confidence are high, as the incident tends to fall within the public's expectations.

An Incident Triggering a Crisis

If, for example, a telephone emergency call is mishandled making an incident far worse than it had to be, and if it wasn't the first time that such an allegation was made, then that can trigger political action from City Council, protests from community groups, angry denunciations and calls for investigations and firings. Before you know it that simple incident can snowball into something which moves beyond the direct ability of an organization to manage. This incident escalates into something which will not easily go away and the resolution of the incident is no longer within the power of the organization. The incident can instantly trigger a crisis.

Emergency Response (Quadrant 2)

An emergency is 'an unexpected situation or sudden occurrence of a serious and urgent nature that demands immediate action'. It is also defined as 'a pressing need, as after a flood, for relief or help; a state of emergency'. (*Webster's Dictionary*)

A major marine spill, a significant flooding, an evacuation, a train derailment, a damaging financial report, are not minor or daily incidents. They require an emergency response with significant resources. If the public and the media's focus is limited to 24 to 48 hours, then it usually qualifies as an emergency response. In the emergency response mode, control is low but confidence remains high.

Emergency Management (Quadrant 3)

Any response time longer than 48 to 72 hours moves the issue into emergency management mode. Again, it is not a crisis. It tests the capabilities of not only the responsible organization, but the professionals who handle it who are paid to do so and, if allowed to do the job, can handle it. Potential vulnerabilities will surface wherever the weak links are located. If, for example, a major marine spill requires several public and private agencies and companies to work smoothly as a team, and they fail to do so, then that can have a significant effect on the perception of whether or not the emergency was well handled.

Once the emergency response moves into the emergency management phase, then confidence starts to decline. The longer the emergency management phase continues, the further confidence levels drop despite the fact that control of the situation is retained.

Crisis (Quadrant 4)

A crisis is an event, revelation, allegation or set of circumstances which threatens the integrity, reputation, or survival of an individual or organization.

Alternatively, a crisis is defined as '*an unstable condition* in political, international or economic affairs in which an abrupt or decisive change is impending.' (Webster's Dictionary)

The scope of the event or issue may be so wide and so significant that it completely overtakes all other operations of the organization during the period in question. In a crisis, confidence and control are low. The actual or potential damage to the organization is considerable and the organization cannot, or has chosen not to, on its own, put an immediate end to it.

Remember, if a damaging allegation has been made, from a credible source or in a credible media outlet, it does not have to be true in order to be damaging. It must be treated with as much importance as if it were true, because it has the potential to be believed.

Crisis Communications

The process of managing the strategy, messages, timing and distribution channels necessary to communicate effectively with the media, employees, core constituencies, clients, customers and stake holders. The focus of the crisis communications function is to facilitate the rapid de-escalation of the crisis through timely and effective communications methods.

How do you recognize a crisis?

"If you don't know, then you're really in trouble."

Actually, this question is not as simple as it initially sounds. Some organizations are so determined to be seen as managing a crisis, that they are in a semi-permanent state of constant crisis. Organizations can also be guilty of under-estimating the damage that an incident or allegation can cause them — especially in the court of public opinion.

The two most common mistakes are:
- to misunderstand the nature and scope of an event or issue, or
- to take ownership of an issue that is not yours.

If the Incident is...	The issue could escalate into...
an unexpected loss or deficit	incompetence; cover-up
record profits while massive layoff notices are issued	corporate greed
a tunnel collapse	inept politicians and bureaucrats

To Contain Daily Incidents There Must Be:

- a capable and timely response;
- an admission of error, if appropriate, and
- an open process, subject to public or peer review.

As well, the issue must be the incident itself; not the handling of it, the communications surrounding it, nor the unexpected or unplanned consequences of the incident.

The Role of the Risk and Crisis Communicator

Issues which involve crisis or risk to the public or to customers, clients, shareholders, communities and others must be managed in a highly professional way. The role of the communicator in support of the management of the issue must be equally sophisticated.

When we hear the word 'communications', the normal image of "spin doctors" firing out messages, reams of information and manipulating the media spring all too easily to mind. Today, however, there are new roles for the senior communicator to play - namely that of a **facilitator** and an **integrator**. Ultimately the goals of communications in support of either risk or crisis management are to:
- influence the behavior of stakeholders, and
- to gain credibility.

The Facilitator's Role

In order for communities and other stakeholders to feel a stake in the outcome, they have to have a stake in the process. In order to feel involved in the process, there needs to be the following components:
1) a process which is coherent and accessible;
2) an invitation and a range of options for involvement, and
3) someone to facilitate the process so that the public can be fully informed of needed information, share their views with others, receive intelligent feedback on their contributions and, have an equal chance to be listened to.

The Integrator's Role

In managing risk issues and crises, traditionally most of the energy goes into getting input - and in most cases, rightly so. However, the increasingly difficult challenge is to integrate the findings so that the process moves forward. This is essential. Otherwise opposing sides dig in and nobody learns anything. The communicator must develop skills which are integrative by nature:
1) find common ground among divergent views;
2) establish principles upon which to decide objectively and fairly;
3) develop phenomenal listening skills - to listen to what people are trying to say, to listen for the underlying and often unspoken motive or fear, to get beyond the yelling, emotion and name-calling and encourage people to be constructive, and
4) organize your thinking - to bring order out of chaos and focus to the debate.

Risk

Strategies and techniques for managing the communications of risk issues.

- *factors affecting acceptability*
- *additional cautions*
- *3 guiding principles*
- *risk management decision process*
- *goals of risk communications program*
- *risk communications program*

Public Perception of Risk

Public tends to:
- overestimate the occurrence of rare incidents, and
- underestimate the frequency of common incidents.

Factors Affecting Public Acceptability of Risk

1. Do people have a choice? Who gets to decide?
2. Familiar products, such as household consumer products are more acceptable than, for example, polypropylene.
3. If the public's memory banks are filled with similar or linked public health disasters (tainted blood supply) then the outrage will be all the higher.
4. The relative relationship between the "perpetrators" and the "victims" can have an enormous impact upon the acceptability of risks. The old cliche of the "little guy" battling city hall (or big corporation) still has a phenomenal media play to it. When the risks apparently outweigh the benefits then it plays even more strongly into the sense of unfairness underlying the issue.

© 1996 *McLoughlin MultiMedia Publishing Ltd.*

What to Watch Out For

1. Risk-benefit analysis should be handled extremely delicately. Any contamination or degradation of environmental or health standards tends to trigger moral outrage.
2. Actions do speak louder than words. Trust is built over time by concrete actions not smooth words. Acting quickly and responsibly does not mean you are admitting responsibility in a legal sense.
3. Just because the public is 'non-expert' doesn't mean they are stupid. Even though the actual hazard may be relatively inconsequential, it doesn't mean that people can't become outraged nevertheless. If the hazard level is low, the risk can still be significant in the public's view.
4. When the sense of indignation is high, the public may not be listening to dry numbers and statistics. You could find yourself on a totally different plane from the public. You could be talking facts and they could be talking the language of morals- "power", "greed", "control". So in order to be heard, the sense of outrage must be reduced.
5. Make all the numbers available. Don't hide anything or trust will drop even lower.
6. Find out what people want to know and then provide it to them quickly and accurately.
7. Even though some of the issues are dry and technical, risk in the public domain deals with "caring", "choice", and "sharing" - all soft words, but nonetheless powerful.

8. Use comparisons to explain the numbers and put them in the context of people's lives.
9. Risk communicators should seek to involve people in order to deal with perceptions of bureaucracy or remoteness.

Conclusion

Think of the pressures to open communications with the public - not so much as an obligation, but as an opportunity to build relationships which can be mutually beneficial.

3 Guiding Principles For Risk Communications

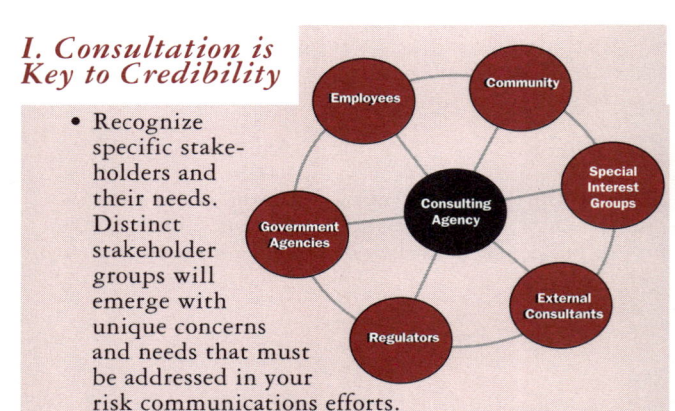

I. Consultation is Key to Credibility

- Recognize specific stakeholders and their needs. Distinct stakeholder groups will emerge with unique concerns and needs that must be addressed in your risk communications efforts.
- A comprehensive consultation plan is essential. If you can get "buy-in" for the plan from internal staff, external consultants and stakeholders, the entire process will run more smoothly.
- To be credible, a consultation process must be seen as fair. It must be clear (and it must be true) that you are interested in what stakeholders have to say.
- Show the public that you are serious about their involvement. Listening and responding to the public's concerns are as important as the content of your messages.
- Get parties to listen to one another. If you don't, public understanding and consensus building will prove difficult to achieve.

II. Communications Must be Open and Coherent

- In communicating risk issues, focus not only on the dangers posed by the risk but also on the opportunities the situation offers to engage the public in a learning process.
- Communications efforts and consultation strategies should seek to achieve consensus. Consensus may not always be achieved but the process should strive for it.
- Communicate early and often. Be visible. Don't allow a vacuum of information to be created as others will move in to fill it, or at the very least, emotions will tend to dominate the public discourse.
- A significant effort to promote informed consent and shared decision-making among stakeholders can build public support for accepting reasonable levels of risk.
- Be honest. Tell the public what you know and what you don't know.
- Independent third party support enhances credibility. The less political the source, the more believable. Where appropriate, consider hiring outside, respected consultants who would report directly to stakeholders.
- Inevitably, old issues change and new issues emerge. Be pro-active rather that reactive by trying to anticipate how issues might evolve.
- Short term victories at the expense of full disclosure can undermine your credibility permanently. Think long term.

- Both "expert" ("objective", "rational") and "non-expert" ("subjective") language are legitimate and are entitled to receive equal public respect.

III. Understanding Risk Perception is Essential

- Perceived risk often differs dramatically from risk as measured objectively. Find out how your stakeholders view the risk, and take this into account when you communicate with them.
- When the public is worried, don't ignore it. Never tell the public that they "shouldn't worry." Rather, try to discover the sources of the worry.
- Orient the communication effort around building understanding of risks.
- Work with the media on the presentation of risk through seminars and pro-active initiatives so that when issues arise there will be more context built into the stories and more evenhanded coverage.

Public Perception and Expectations

- Risk communications also deals with public perception. If the public perceives a chemical as highly toxic, then they will act on that perception.
- Another factor in shaping public reactions to risk issues is expectations. If the public's expectation is that there should be zero risk associated with an initiative, a product or a process then they will respond with that expectation clearly at the forefront of their minds.
- Managing both perception and expectations is key to gaining understanding and support.

Risk Management Decision Process

1. Initiation
2. Preliminary Analysis
3. Risk Estimation
4. Risk Evaluation
5. Risk Control and Financing
6. Action
7. Monitoring and Evaluation

Build your risk communications strategy on the risk management framework known as the Q850 Risk Management Decision Process* which is internationally recognized. Otherwise, the communications efforts will be de-coupled from the risk management process itself, and thus rendered ineffective.

* *Canadian Standards Association, 1995.*

The Goals of a Risk Communications Program

Create a risk communications program based on goals which can be evaluated.

Focus your communications steps around identifying and listening to stakeholders, providing information, moving towards shared understanding of the risks and consequences, developing shared goals and accepting principles which underlie selected the risk control option. The ultimate outcome is to achieve consensus behind the decision. Re-affirmation of the public's decision is important to ensure comfort level with original decision.

The Goals of a Risk Communications Program

Identifying, Listening and Providing Information → Shared Understanding of Risks and Consequences → Development of Shared Goals → Acceptance of Principles → Achieving Consensus Behind Decision

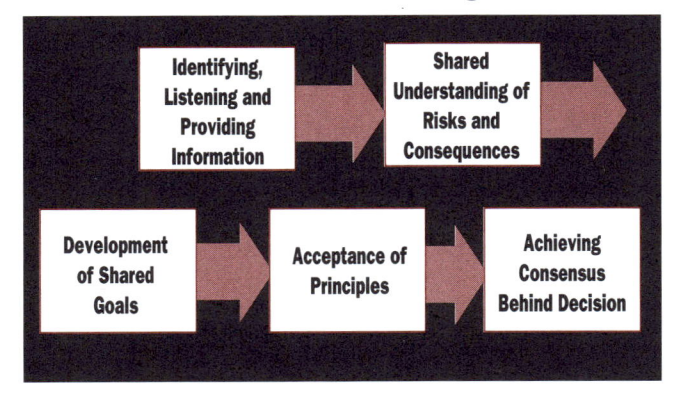

Risk Communications Program

Step One: Initiation

- Sources of potential danger are identified and characterized.
- Responsibilities are assigned.
- Potential stakeholders are identified.

Risk Communications Program Activities

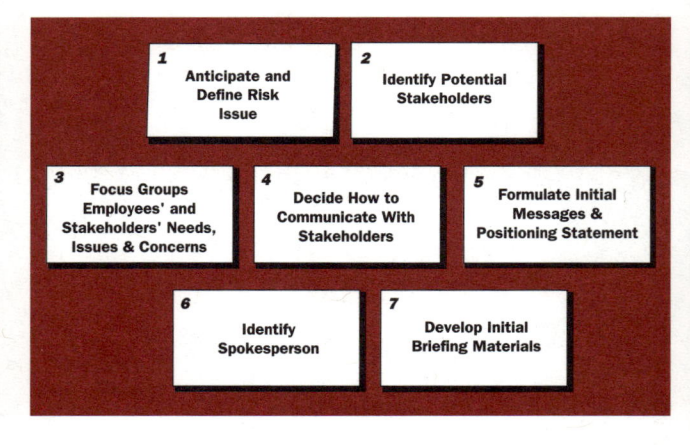

1. Anticipate and Define Risk Issue
2. Identify Potential Stakeholders
3. Focus Groups Employees' and Stakeholders' Needs, Issues & Concerns
4. Decide How to Communicate With Stakeholders
5. Formulate Initial Messages & Positioning Statement
6. Identify Spokesperson
7. Develop Initial Briefing Materials

Audiences or Stakeholders

(those who have a stake in either the process or the outcome)

1. Employees and their families.
2. Retired employees and suppliers.
3. Immediate neighbors/community.
4. Emergency response personnel.
5. Environmental groups and individual activists.
6. Health care providers and professionals.
7. Small business groups and associations.
8. Senior citizens, others with special needs.
9. Government agencies at all levels.
10. Political leaders.
11. Opinion leaders - columnists, commentators, high-profile community leaders.
12. Volunteer groups.
13. Schools, universities.
14. Media.

Establishing a Dialogue with the Audiences

Facilitating an on-going dialogue is essential to develop community understanding about the relative risks associated with the plant emissions, or low-level radiation questions surrounding power lines or the risk to the community of paroled offenders or clients with special needs. Quantifying such risks is one of the great challenges in risk communications.

Employee Communications

Always begin your communications efforts on risk issues with your employees. They can often be your harshest critics and will play a vital role in the credibility of the external communications efforts. Employees can also flag issues on the horizon, in effect, acting as an early warning signal. They can also be the organization's best ambassadors if they are well informed, as they can help in community liaison efforts.

Community Relations

Community relations is particularly important when the risk issue is specific to a work site or a plant. The community which is immediately adjacent to or potentially affected by the processes undertaken at the plant will usually play the most significant role in determining whether or not the risk communications program will be successful.

Plant managers, hospital administrators, community group homes, for example, are learning the benefits of working more closely with community leaders, neighborhood spokespersons, small business owners and residents, emergency personnel, medical and environmental specialists etc.

One key method to develop effective liaison, is to create a community liaison group (CLG) made up of a representative committee tasked with building communications between the consulting organization and the community.

Step Two: Preliminary Analysis

- The scope of the decision is defined.
- Stakeholder analysis begins.
- Update of risk information database.
- Risk scenarios are used to identify possible exposure.
- Consultation strategy is designed.

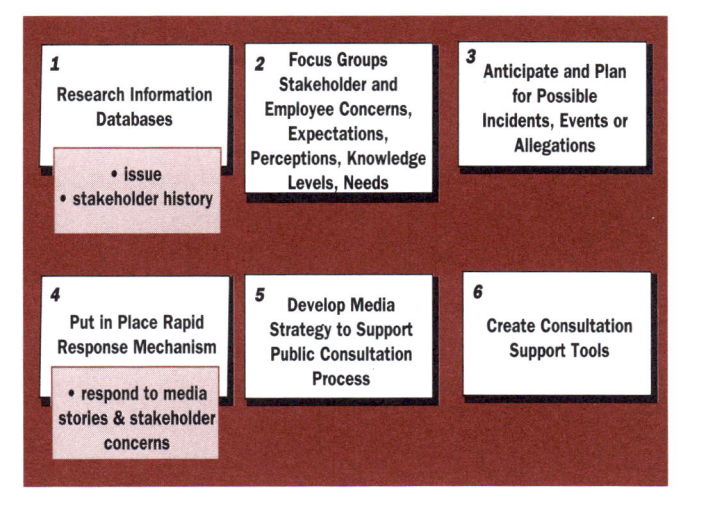

1 **Research Information Databases** • issue • stakeholder history	2 **Focus Groups Stakeholder and Employee Concerns, Expectations, Perceptions, Knowledge Levels, Needs**	3 **Anticipate and Plan for Possible Incidents, Events or Allegations**
4 **Put in Place Rapid Response Mechanism** • respond to media stories & stakeholder concerns	5 **Develop Media Strategy to Support Public Consultation Process**	6 **Create Consultation Support Tools**

Risk Communications Program Activities

Database Research

Developing an active on-going database is essential to anticipating risk issues. Electronic on-line databases are flourishing. Among them:
- Lexis®-Nexis® database called ClientSmart, which is tailored for public relations and communications specialists. A specific issue or topic can be tracked and saved.
- CompuServe has the Executive News Service (Go ENS).
- World Wide Web sites include:
  - www.infosage.ibm.com
  - www.newspage.com
  - www.infoseek.com
- A range of issue-tracking tools can be accessed through America On-Line (AOL).

Effective Messages

Messages are not just a series of one-liners. Instead, effective messages emerge from a process which begins with:
- the goals you are trying to achieve;
- the needs of your target audiences, and
- an appropriate framing for the messages.

The Communicate with Power Message Developer™ offers an organized process to develop messages.

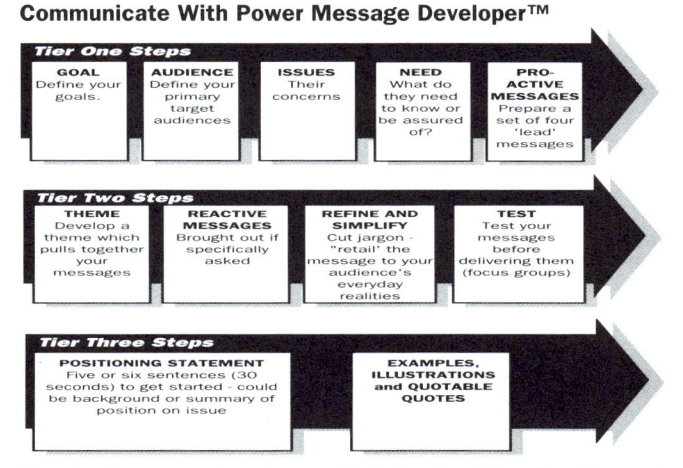

Communicate With Power Message Developer™

Tier One Steps

GOAL	AUDIENCE	ISSUES	NEED	PRO-ACTIVE MESSAGES
Define your goals.	Define your primary target audiences	Their concerns	What do they need to know or be assured of?	Prepare a set of four 'lead' messages

Tier Two Steps

THEME	REACTIVE MESSAGES	REFINE AND SIMPLIFY	TEST
Develop a theme which pulls together your messages	Brought out if specifically asked	Cut jargon - "retail" the message to your audience's everyday realities	Test your messages before delivering them (focus groups)

Tier Three Steps

POSITIONING STATEMENT	EXAMPLES, ILLUSTRATIONS and QUOTABLE QUOTES
Five or six sentences (30 seconds) to get started - could be background or summary of position on issue	

See the Encountering the Media® Pocket Tips Booklet and software program for details.

© 1996 *McLoughlin MultiMedia Publishing Ltd.*

Making Your Messages Memorable

- Keep your messages simple. Remember, on television 60% of the messages emerge from non-verbal sources, 37% from tone and attitude and 3% of the messages come from verbal sources.
- The more senses you involve the greater the understanding. Words alone are usually not enough.

According to the U.S. Bureau of Advertising, people remember:
- 10% of what they read
- 20% of what they hear
- 30% of what they see
- 50% of what they see and hear

As well, color visuals increase learning attention and recall by 55% to 78%.

What Works

1. Snapshots of two exact situations - separated by time or location.
2. Contrast actual performance with recognized standard (by regulator or national or international body).
3. Compare risks of action with risks of inaction.
4. Compare optional solutions.
5. Compare with same risks in different locations.
6. Compare estimates.

How Not to Communicate Numbers

- Don't compare involuntary risk numbers to voluntary risk situations (radiation exposure vs. cigarette smoking).
- Don't mix apples and oranges - use the same basis for comparison.
- Don't use numbers that people can't relate to - "parts per trillion" vs. "one pea in a mountain of peas the size of Mount Everest".

Needs

What do your target audiences need? Do they want to be consulted before decisions are made or actions are taken? Are they looking for information to help them make informed decisions? Find out.

Messages are more likely to…	If they…
gain attention	• survive editing by media • use memorable phrases • are not buried by too many words and a barrage of messages • are communicated dynamically • are supported by visuals or backdrop/setting that complement the message
be understood	• use simple words • are relevant to the lives of your target audiences
be believed	• come from an organization with a good reputation • are delivered by a credible communicator • are communicated in a direct manner with sincerity • are spoken objectively with compassion and caring • are delivered with a nonpartisan approach
be acted upon by your target audience	• include clear directions • are followed-up with communications that are consistent, clear and frequent • are delivered to a target audience prepared with the knowledge and tools to act • are repeated by those with influence over your audience

Step Three: Risk Estimation

- Frequency of risk scenarios are identified along with estimate of their consequences.
- Stakeholder analysis is refined.
- Risk Information Base is updated.
- Consultation Program is initiated.

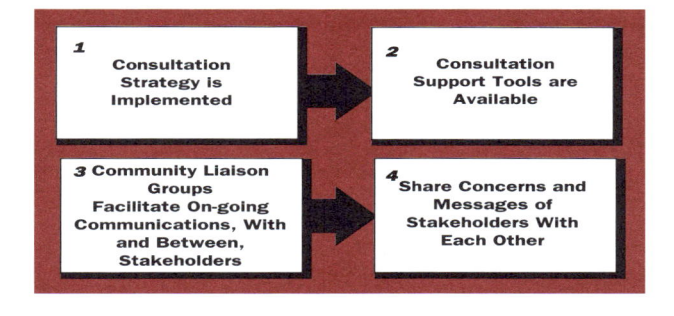

Risk Communications Program Activities

1. Consultation Strategy is Implemented
2. Consultation Support Tools are Available
3. Community Liaison Groups Facilitate On-going Communications, With and Between, Stakeholders
4. Share Concerns and Messages of Stakeholders With Each Other

Step Four: Risk Evaluation

- Benefits and costs are estimated and integrated.
- Stakeholder acceptability of risk options is assessed.
- Risk information base is updated by team.

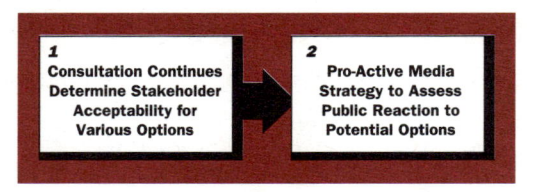

Risk Communications Program Activities

1 Consultation Continues Determine Stakeholder Acceptability for Various Options → **2** Pro-Active Media Strategy to Assess Public Reaction to Potential Options

Step Five: Risk Control and Financing

- Feasibility of risk control options are identified.
- Control options are evaluated for effectiveness, cost and risks.

Risk Communications Program Activities

1 Consultation Focused on Risk Control Options	2 Preparation of Briefing Materials	3 Referenda, public hearings, town hall meetings to assess acceptability of preferred option
4 Scientific Studies and Reports are Shared Among All Stakeholders	5 Media Interviews Undertaken by Key Team Members to Clarify Facts	6 Stakeholder Views of Residual Risk are Received and Assessed

Step Six: Action

- Chosen risk decision is announced and implemented.

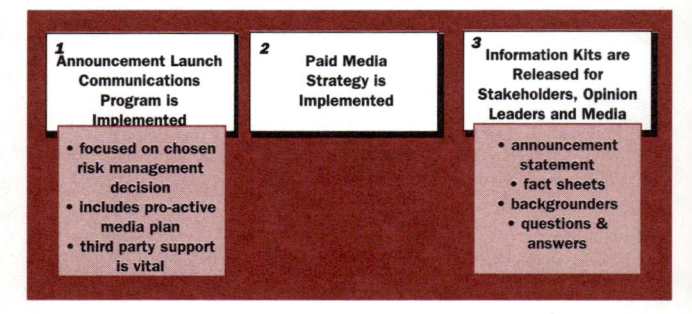

Risk Communications Program Activities

1. Announcement Launch Communications Program is Implemented
- focused on chosen risk management decision
- includes pro-active media plan
- third party support is vital

2. Paid Media Strategy is Implemented

3. Information Kits are Released for Stakeholders, Opinion Leaders and Media
- announcement statement
- fact sheets
- backgrounders
- questions & answers

Step Seven: Monitoring and Evaluation

- Monitoring mechanisms are implemented.
- Overall risk management program is evaluated.
- Results are shared and plugged in.

Risk Communications Program Activities

1 Conduct Polling to Gauge Public Reactions, Behavior and Attitudes	2 Focus Groups Fine Tune and Re-Work Messages and/or Advertising as Required	3 Step Up Political Liaison Program
4 Trouble-Shooting as Required	5 Analyze Media Coverage to Determine Trends	6 Communicate Findings Internally & Externally and Flag Emerging or Potential Issues

Risk Communications Program Critical Path - Part I

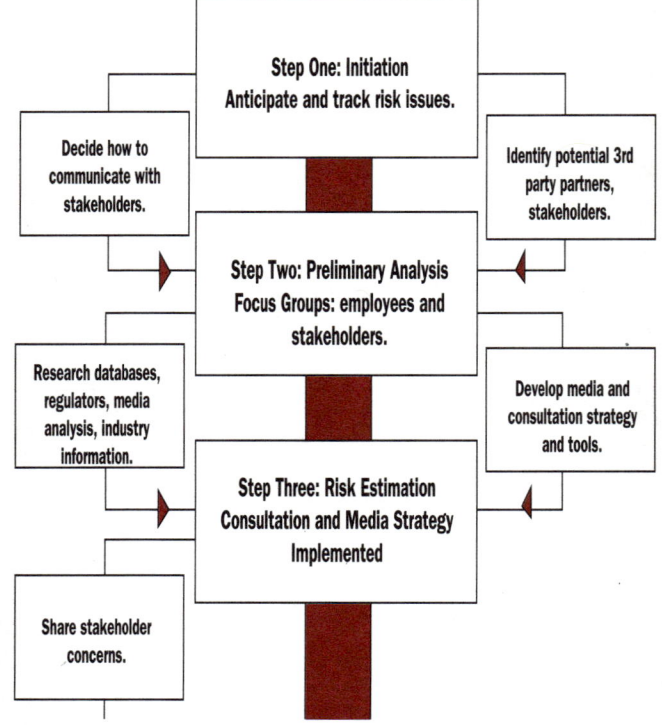

Step One: Initiation
Anticipate and track risk issues.

Decide how to communicate with stakeholders.

Identify potential 3rd party partners, stakeholders.

Step Two: Preliminary Analysis
Focus Groups: employees and stakeholders.

Research databases, regulators, media analysis, industry information.

Develop media and consultation strategy and tools.

Step Three: Risk Estimation
Consultation and Media Strategy Implemented

Share stakeholder concerns.

Note: The critical path is down the center. Delays matter in the process only when they are on, or when they reach, the critical path.

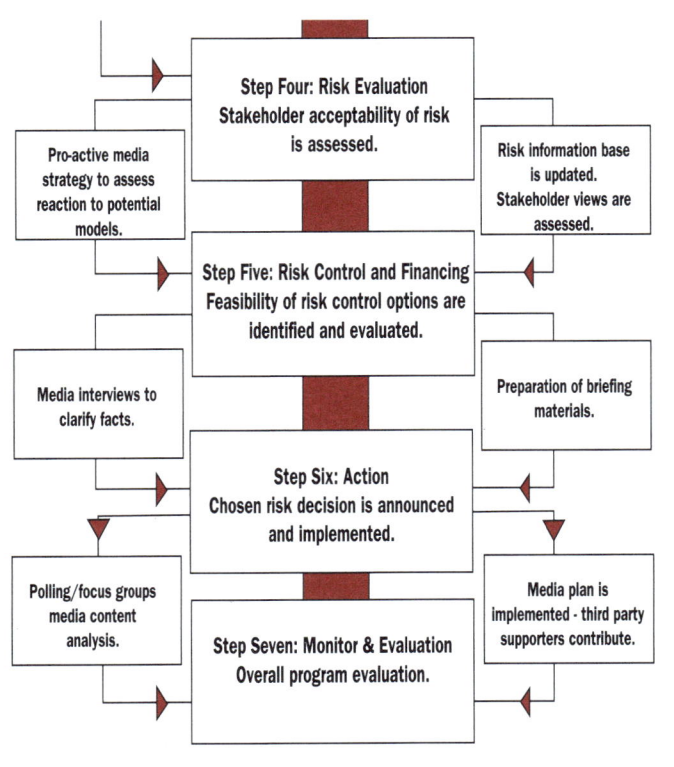

Risk Communications Program Critical Path - Part II

Step Four: Risk Evaluation
Stakeholder acceptability of risk is assessed.

- Pro-active media strategy to assess reaction to potential models.
- Risk information base is updated. Stakeholder views are assessed.

Step Five: Risk Control and Financing
Feasibility of risk control options are identified and evaluated.

- Media interviews to clarify facts.
- Preparation of briefing materials.

Step Six: Action
Chosen risk decision is announced and implemented.

- Polling/focus groups media content analysis.
- Media plan is implemented - third party supporters contribute.

Step Seven: Monitor & Evaluation
Overall program evaluation.

Risk Communications Verbals, Para-Verbals and Non-Verbals

Overall Tips

- demonstrate caring
- listen more than you speak
- communicate clearly using terms your audience understands
- step out of "government bureaucrat" or "corporate spokesperson" stereotype
- communicate on a "person- to- person" basis, using an intimate, down-to-earth approach
- remember that while you probably judge yourself by your intentions; your audience will judge you by your actions
- your behavior must convey your intentions
- make sure that your non-verbal communications support what you are saying
- actions speak louder than words, so 'walk the talk'
- note that when trust is low and public concern is high, non-verbal communication tends to dominate the impact of the message itself

Communicating During a Public Meeting

(See details in the Making Effective Presentations Pocket Tips Booklet.)

If a public hearing or consultation meeting with stakeholders is arranged, it requires planning, preparation, focus and discipline in order to maximize its benefits.

Planning

- Decide on consultation strategy, timing and location.
- Decide on appropriate stakeholder groups and expert witnesses to invite.
- Send invitations to stakeholders and expert witnesses.
- Develop a schedule for appearances by all witnesses.
- Develop a media advisory/news release.

Listening

- Listen actively: which means strong eye contact, support the presenter's attempt to express herself; convey open body language - relaxed; open and animated face.
- Build in pauses - don't interrupt the presenter; never signal impatience.
- Consider thoughtfully the feelings behind the words - don't just react to the words chosen by the individual.

Responding to Comments

- Begin with an empathetic comment such as "I understand why you are concerned."
- Be supportive. Don't create an overly confrontational atmosphere.
- Allow a certain amount of venting; thank those who do for their views and move on.
- Ask questions in a neutral way, always seeking to clarify meanings.

Paraphrasing

- Reflect to others what they have just said in an attempt to capture the accurate meaning.
- Serves to emphasize the most important points.
- Determine accuracy of your understanding.

Summarize

- Feeds back what has been said over the length of the discussion.
- Puts the presentation into perspective.
- Can reflect the feelings of the group in a structured way.
- Also demonstrates that you have been listening.

Most importantly, good communicators must be credible.

A Credible Spokesperson:

- Communicates caring, empathy, honesty and sincerity, the ability to relate.
- Has the credentials (academic and other experience) valued by the target audience.
- Is someone to whom the target audience can relate - a shared background; someone who brings everyday life experience to the issue.
- Expresses a mix of compassion and sincerity with a reasonable tone. One who doesn't communicate "uptight", "rigid" characteristics but whose personality comes across as relaxed and calm.
- Is fairly senior - not necessarily the C.E.O. or Agency Head but should be recognized as a major influence in the decision making and is accountable to the public for the actions of his or her institution.
- Is connected to the communities represented by stakeholders.

Quick Tips for Risk Communications

1. Involve the public as a legitimate partner in decisions.
2. Plan and evaluate your efforts.
3. Be honest, open and direct.
4. Share information.
5. Respond to expressed feelings.
6. Follow-up.
7. Admit your mistakes.
8. When you are uncertain, don't pretend to be certain.
9. Speak in plain language. Choose your vocabulary carefully. Avoid words like "safe, always, never, guarantee".
10. Don't be a "bureaucrat" or a "corporate-type".
11. Keep in constant contact with other organizations who have a stake in the issue. Meet regularly and share information.
12. Make sure your representatives are good communicators and are trained.
13. Anticipate and meet the needs of the media.
14. Don't speculate or guess.
15. Don't make promises you can't keep.

Communicate With Power Risk Communications Planner™

	Stakeholder 1	Stakeholder 2	Stakeholder 3
	Local community	Pulp & paper industry	Environmental groups
Why this stakeholder?	Potential impacts on environment & possible job loss	Economic stake	Environmental consequences
Risk perception focus	Concern about environmental impact	Concern that risk is being over-stated	Serious potential damage to air, water and fish habitat
Communications tools	Information kit Questionnaire Invitation	Backgrounder Invitation	Information kit Invitation
Consultation Models/Support Tools	Community Liaison Group (CLG) Kiosk at fair Meetings Letters Ads in Weeklies	Hearings Meetings	Hearings Meetings Letters
Responsibility	Risk Management team - Lead Communications - Support	Risk Management Team Communications - Coordinate	Scientific team - Lead Communications - Support
Time Frame	May-June	July-Sept.	July-Sept.
Message	We want your input	The process will be fair	We will follow all environmental regulations - your input is needed

© 1996 McLoughlin MultiMedia Publishing Ltd.

Public Consultations

- *why consult?*
- *developing a consultation process*
- *when to hold consultations*
- *consultation models*
- *information loop*

Why Consult?

Without an effective consultation process, risk management decisions have little legitimacy. If an organization with a vested stake in the risk issue promotes a specific initiative or course of events, it is open to widespread criticism of being self-serving or biased.

Consultation creates an opportunity for the public to be involved in the process. Involvement in the process creates an increased sense of ownership about the outcome.

Consultation Goals

1. To disseminate information to stakeholders.
2. To receive input into the risk management process.
3. To be seen to be listening as well as to listen.
4. To build consensus behind the ultimate decision.

Making the Case for Consultations

There is, at times, a resistance in some quarters to consultations. Resisters often argue "why raise the profile of the issue?" or "aren't we going to create resistance?" While these are legitimate questions, it is important to recognize that there are significant consequences if you don't consult:
- stakeholder commitment will be more difficult;
- widespread, more thoughtful points of view and feedback may be drowned out by narrow, well-financed special interests;
- access to data and studies may be curtailed;
- trust and confidence among all parties may never develop, and
- it can affect the credibility of the initiative.

Effective Consultation Means...

1. Increased stakeholder input into decision-making. The input includes facts and their perceptions concerning the level of risk and the perceived impacts.
2. Greater understanding by stakeholders of risk management issues and processes.
3. Shared understanding. This leads to shared goals for dealing with the risk issues.
4. Shared goals which lead to acceptance of common principles for decision-making.
5. Building buy-in of the risk management processes through effective two-way communications. This can lead to buy-in of the outcome.
6. Stakeholders will be less likely to be swayed by scare tactics or by those who wish to derail the process.

Ten Keys to Developing a Consultation Process

1. Invest the time to do it right. If consultation is effective it will save time and money by avoiding prolonged stakeholder resistance.
2. Develop a consultation plan which identifies:
   - the stakeholders to be consulted;
   - why you want to consult with them (purely advisory or a share in decision-making authority?);
   - when you plan to consult them, and
   - the range of stakeholder consultation initiatives you plan to take at each stage in the risk management process.
3. Identify and seek stakeholder input into the formulation of the objectives, processes and principles behind the consultation.
4. Get stakeholder commitment to the objectives, principles and processes.

5. Gather data and studies early on as they are integral to the efficiency and effectiveness of the process.
6. Start the consultations as early as possible in the risk analysis process in order to generate buy-in of the process and ultimately the decisions made.
7. Commit to providing stakeholders access to the studies and data which affect risk decisions, except where release of such information violates security, privacy or confidentiality.
8. Communicate both positive and negative aspects of the issue in a neutral manner.
9. Provide feedback on the results at each stage of the consultation.
10. Develop a media relations plan which supports the goals of the consultation.

When to Hold Public Consultations

Hold a consultation if...

- there is a reasonable possibility that the results can affect the decision
- there is sufficient time and resources to conduct the consultation properly

Don't hold a consultation if...

- there is an urgent need for immediate action
- the issue is almost entirely technical, trivial or routine
- there is no intention to allow the risk decisions to be influenced by stakeholder input

Decide if the issue is important enough to conduct consultations. The time frame to hold consultations is based on the urgency for action. It will be key in determining the appropriate consultation mechanism. The more time available for consultation, the wider the range of options.

Communicate With Power Public Consultation Decision-Maker™

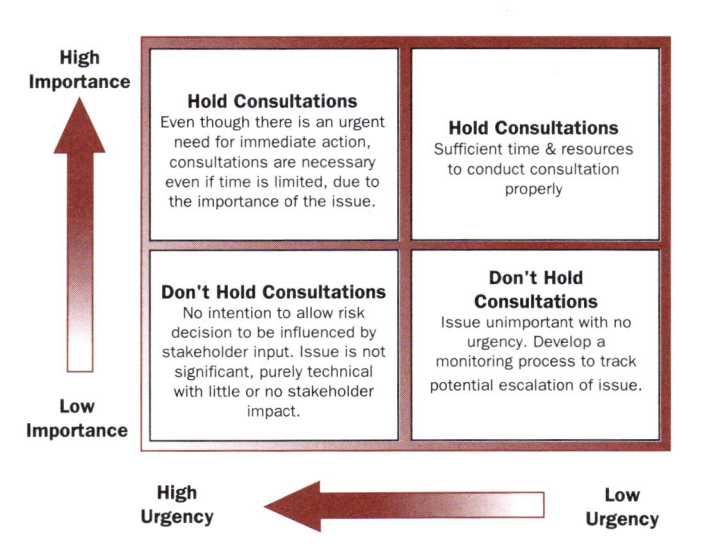

High Importance ↑

Hold Consultations Even though there is an urgent need for immediate action, consultations are necessary even if time is limited, due to the importance of the issue.	**Hold Consultations** Sufficient time & resources to conduct consultation properly
Don't Hold Consultations No intention to allow risk decision to be influenced by stakeholder input. Issue is not significant, purely technical with little or no stakeholder impact.	**Don't Hold Consultations** Issue unimportant with no urgency. Develop a monitoring process to track potential escalation of issue.

Low Importance

High Urgency ← **Low Urgency**

© 1996 McLoughlin MultiMedia Publishing Ltd.

Consultation Models

A variety of consultation models can be appropriate to any risk issue and may be required over the course of the risk management process.

Take into consideration the following variables:
- the objective - ranging from advice only to decision-making by the stakeholders;
- the subject of the consultation - ranging from technical decisions to emotionally-loaded issues with widespread public or community implications;
- the number of stakeholder groups and people affected - the more involved, the greater the requirement and range of options;
- the level of knowledge for each stakeholder - and how much knowledge is required to meet the consultation objectives;
- the time available - if there is sufficient time to carry out a credible consultation process, and
- the resources - limited resources will curtail the scope and options available for consultation.

Consultation Models and Support Tools

No one consultation model or process is appropriate to all situations. In fact, with each risk issue there will be a requirement to implement a range of consultation mechanisms. The following forms of consultation include some of the most common models:

Consultation Models

1. **Advisory Committees** - Often selected for expert input into risk management processes, advisory bodies can be vital if credibility is challenged. The advisory committee can provide either issue-specific advice or comment on a range of related issues. Ideally, the committee should be representative of expert community members and stakeholders. Ensure that prospective members are respected by their communities or their professions. They can also be utilized in consultation sessions with wider audiences. Usually, advisory committees are formed to advise decision-makers and do not have decision-making authority themselves.
2. **Community Liaison Groups (CLGs)** - The community is asked to appoint representatives (about 10-12) who represent the community in dialogue with the consulting agency or company. Although these groups should not be given veto power, they can play a vital role in influencing the community. Therefore, they should be selected based on their willingness to be open-minded, share their ideas and views and communicate with community members.

3. **Conferences** - Formal meetings of invited representatives of stakeholders who are brought together to discuss and share views on the risk issue. The advantage to a conference's structured environment is that outside experts and stakeholder representatives can provide information in a thoughtful atmosphere. As well, the conference can provide workshops, seminars, tours and social events to help create understanding and build relationships.
4. **Discussion Groups** - One-time-only or, ideally, ongoing opportunities to provide feedback on a discussion paper or to discuss various aspects of the risk issues.
5. **Focus Groups** - Informal discussions facilitated by a neutral individual and attended by a sample of up to 20 representatives of a particular stakeholder group. If there is a desire to test the capability of different groups to develop common ground in their positions, then participants could be selected from a cross-section of different groups.
6. **Hearings** - Formal proceedings in which selected groups are invited to present their views before an appointed body. Hearings are often called to satisfy a legal requirement or a political decision. Stakeholders may be invited to submit either a written opinion or to make a presentation.

7. **Informal Calls and Visits** - Although not strictly considered a consultation model, meeting informally with stakeholders can provide a sounding board before a formal consultation process is undertaken. As they are private and not open to the media, these meetings have no public legitimacy and should be used as a supplement only. They are particularly useful when briefing political leaders and other opinion leaders or for people who are uncomfortable in a public forum.
8. **Public Hearings** - Formally convened, usually by regulatory bodies to hear briefs from interested parties with ultimate goal of deciding the appropriate risk control option.
9. **Questionnaires** - A series of questions related to a specific issue, formulated by the consulting agency, to which respondents are asked to reply. Could be in multiple choice format, conducted over the telephone or in writing. Questionnaires are used to survey or poll random samples of a target group, and thus it is important that the questionnaire is carefully designed and that its administration is standardized.
10. **Referenda** - A referral of a question or proposal to a stakeholder group for a vote. The results of a referendum may or may not be binding upon the sponsoring organization. However, if the results are ignored there can be significantly negative repercussions.

11. **Requests for Briefs** - A written summary of stakeholders' perspectives on an issue. Briefs usually include recommendations for management of the issue.
12. **Stakeholder Meetings** - Conducted either by the consulting organization itself or sponsored by a legitimate neutral third party either in a series of small meetings.
13. **Toll-free telephone lines** - Can be set up to record public comments, listen to a prerecorded message or may be staffed in order to respond directly to comments, questions and concerns. It can also be used to administer a questionnaire.
14. **Town Hall Meetings** - Informal community meeting designed to listen to community concerns. Usually includes presentation by consulting agency.
15. **Computer Bulletin Boards (BBS)** - Invite the public to e-mail in their comments for consideration. They may also input questions and receive a reply.

Support Tools

1. **Advertising/Feedback** - Ads are placed in media outlets to inform the public of plans, studies, initiatives, consultation meetings or to raise awareness of issues. By adding a tear-off coupon or invitation for comments, this tool can elicit significant public reaction. It is particularly useful if time is tight and public input must be sought from as wide a scope as possible.
2. **A/V Presentations** - Outline of known facts, issues to be addressed. No more than 20 minutes in length. Emphasis on visuals.
3. **Computer Bulletin-Boards** - Used to focus discussions in stakeholder meetings. Stakeholders with access to a computer and internet connection may download information such as studies from the consulting agency's web site or bulletin board.
4. **Database Research** - electronic, on-line information, stakeholder groups, industry information, media, etc.
5. **Discussion Papers** - Documents issued by third parties - outside experts and other agencies - which provide background and detail, or outline proposals on key aspects of the risk issue. To encourage stakeholder response, the papers should be tied to consultation initiatives as an opportunity for gaining feedback such as discussion groups, meetings, 1-800 lines or other initiatives.

6. **Drop-in Centers** - Often set up at special events, such as conferences, trade shows, exhibitions or shopping centers. Staffed by the consulting agencies or corporations, these centers provide an informal opportunity for one-on-one dialogue about an issue, either verbally or in writing.
7. **Information Letters or Newsletters** - Regularly sent out to communities; includes background information and/or information updates on how a risk issue of interest to the selected stakeholders is being managed, along with a request for feedback. The letters may also be useful to keep the media abreast of the consultation process (sometimes known as "information-for-file").
8. **Fax-Back Systems** - Designed to provide more detailed information sheets and backgrounders on a series of issues. The public can call in and are prompted through a series of steps to instantly receive, by fax, the information they desire.
9. **Media Interviews** - Designed to demonstrate responsiveness, provide information and communicate caring.

The Communicate with Power Consultation Loop™

The agency rolls out its consultation initiatives with a series of models and tools in order to generate public dialogue with and among stakeholders. The information from the roll out is processed, fed back and shared among all participants.

The Communicate With Power Consultation Loop™

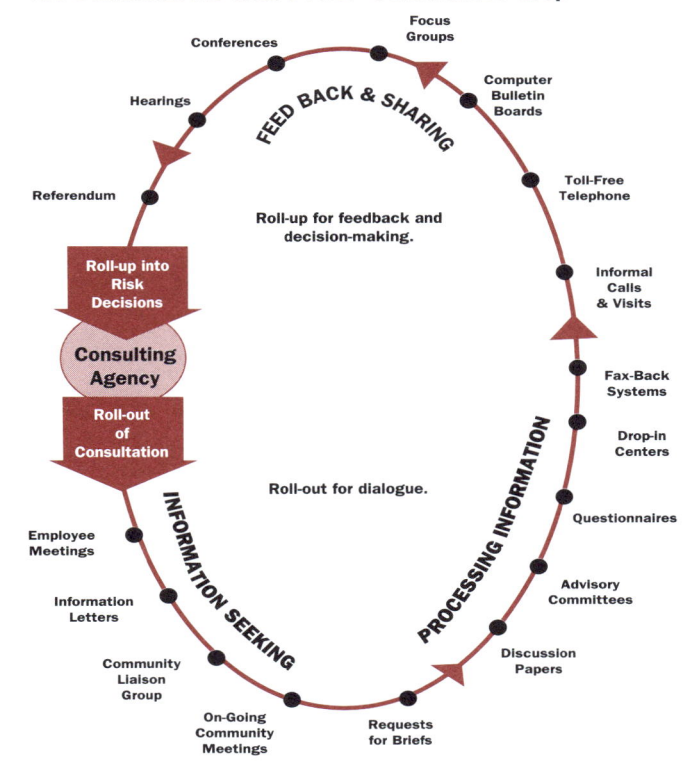

FEED BACK & SHARING

- Focus Groups
- Conferences
- Computer Bulletin Boards
- Hearings
- Toll-Free Telephone
- Referendum

Roll-up for feedback and decision-making.

Roll-up into Risk Decisions

Consulting Agency

Roll-out of Consultation

Roll-out for dialogue.

PROCESSING INFORMATION

- Informal Calls & Visits
- Fax-Back Systems
- Drop-in Centers
- Questionnaires
- Advisory Committees
- Discussion Papers

INFORMATION SEEKING

- Employee Meetings
- Information Letters
- Community Liaison Group
- On-Going Community Meetings
- Requests for Briefs

© 1996 McLoughlin MultiMedia Publishing Ltd.

Emergency

- *emergency response*
- *the role of initial responders*
- *emergency management*
- *briefings*

Emergency Response

The power of television to cover an emergency live in all its detail means that as you are responding the public is deciding if you are handling it competently. Their judgments can be very harsh and damaging. It is vital to focus on reaching out through the media to keep the public informed of what you are doing, what your options are and why you have acted the way you have.

Even though a lot of resources have gone into an emergency response or emergency management, you are not necessarily in a crisis. If your organization is handling the emergency well, then you still have credibility. In fact, your credibility can be enhanced by the capability that you are demonstrating as you handle the emergency.

Features of an Emergency

An incident is an emergency if:
- event isn't instantly brought under control;
- impact on environment, public health and safety is increased beyond moderate level;
- there is impact on organization's reputation;
- there is involvement from the regulator or government agencies, and
- there is increased media coverage beyond local focus.

Communicator's Responsibilities:

- roll-out emergency communications plan;
- execute media response and pro-active media plan, and
- bring in additional resources as required.

Emergency Response - Communications Focus

The communications focus in an emergency response is geared to several key roles:

- **Inform the public and key stakeholders,** such as regulators, partners, customers, suppliers, local, state and federal officials and politicians.
- **Anticipate and meet the needs of journalists.**
- **Set up and operate the public input channels,** such as toll-free phone lines, on-line communications, fax-back systems, public meetings.
- **Ensure the organization is visible throughout the process**. Silence and invisibility are signs of unwillingness, incompetence and fear which undermines the perception that the emergency is under control.
- **Manage the message.** Keep the messages clear, honest and consistent. If your message is patently false, premature, or unsupportable by readily available facts, then don't say it.
- **Manage the perception of competence** as well as the reality. The media and the public react primarily on perceptions - of competence, truth, openness etc. If you are not communicating those values then the opposite perception can take hold. If a negative perception takes hold early in the emergency response, then it is very difficult to shake.
- **Ensure that inaccurate or misleading reporting is corrected immediately.**

- **Communicate internally before you make public statements.** Otherwise chaos will truly reign and morale will sink even deeper; thus undermining the quality of the response.
- **Stay in contact with victims' families.** If they get all their news first from the media, then their trust in your abilities and honesty rapidly erode.
- **Ensure that all the news, good or bad, is communicated as soon as you can confirm it;** and that if there is bad news, that it gets out all at once - to all media at the same time. Don't make a public "strip-tease" of bad news. That's how media "feeding frenzies" are developed.
- **Keep the emergency response team fully apprised** of public, media and stakeholder responses so that they are not operating in a vacuum.

The Role of Initial Responders in an Emergency

If a major facility experiences an explosion, a fire or a significant event, early hours communications teams or initial responders, can play a significant role in determining whether or not the organization is seen to be handling the emergency credibly.

The communications role of the initial responder is by definition very limited, but it must be very disciplined in execution. In an emergency at a major facility, the media may well have arrived at the site as a result of monitoring the emergency bands or in response to calls from witnesses. Television cameras may be covering the event live, while communications personnel are off-site.

Why Must Initial Responders Make Some Communication Efforts?

- A large information vacuum is created that rumors will fill.
- By cooperating early on, trust is built with the media and the public is reassured that, while everything may not be instantly under control, you are at least addressing the situation in a professional manner.
- Time must be bought before the Crisis Communications Team can be fully employed.

When the Emergency Response Becomes Emergency Management

The danger point for communicators is that the longer the emergency situation continues, the more the media need to be fed and the hungrier they get to fill their filing demands. Then they start looking around for other issues. This is where emergency response moves into the emergency management phase- that is, beyond the initial 48 hour period.

Emergency Response - Communicators' Focus

- Organize media tours for behind-the-scenes insights into the emergency response.
- Provide assistance to meet with witnesses, victims, families etc. By playing a coordinating role, you are able to demonstrate openness and cooperation with the media, which pays off in stories.
- Conduct regular briefings to meet their deadlines and update requirements.
- Provide access to key emergency management personnel without interfering with the handling of the emergency.
- Organize public outreach programs to ensure that in an evacuation families are kept abreast of developments and emergency personnel can communicate directly with them (and be seen to be communicating).

Internal Briefings

Outline of Internal Presentation to Senior Executive Team or Employees Regarding an Incident or Emergency:

1) What happened?
   - simply put, set out the facts;
   - give the basic "tombstone" data:
   - what took place - focus on the key incident which led to the event without getting into the possible cause at this point
   - where did it happen?
   - when did it occur?
   - how serious is it? The extent of the damage, etc.
2) How did it happen?
   - relate the known chronology of events
   - is the cause known?
   - does the cause matter at this point? In other words, will that piece of information change anything in the response strategy?
3) Responsibility
   - who is the owner of the problem?
   - has the owner accepted responsibility?
   - can the owner respond: immediately? in the near future? with a full response?
   - what is the role to be played by each party?

4) Incident Response
   - what is required to respond?
   - what are the assets to respond?
   - what are the gaps in response capability?
   - what actions have been taken?
   - identify: organizational issues to be addressed, the personnel necessary/available, the equipment necessary/available

5) Compensation and Liability Issues
   - what are the legal issues?

6) Likely impacts and reactions:
   - on/by clients or customers
   - on/by indirect customers, taxpayers, stakeholders
   - special interest groups

7) International Issues
   - if relevant

8) Media
    - what is the level of media interest? Be specific: local, regional, national, international? Number of calls, interviews. Presence of media on-sight.
    - where are the media getting their information?
    - have there been factually inaccurate reports? If so, has any attempt been made to correct them?
    - what are the issues on which the media are focusing?
    - what are we doing to address the media issues?
        - fact gathering process
        - identification of spokesperson
        - contact with HQ/regional or district offices
        - written/ spoken statement?
        - fact sheets?
        - news briefing?
        - interviews?

9) Next Briefing
    - who will be involved?
    - what will be addressed?
    - where will it take place?
    - when?

Crisis

- *communicator's responsibilities*
- *6 crisis communications concepts*
- *10 principles of effective crisis communications*
- *crisis communications plan*

The Communicator's Responsibilities in a Crisis

- **Ensure** that the quality of communications itself does not become the issue.
- **Drive** the communications process pro-actively rather than in a merely reactive manner.
- **Maintain** tight control over who speaks on behalf of the organization. Limit all media and public communications to one spokesperson wherever possible.
- **Utilize** the public role of the CEO or the Agency Head to the maximum benefit. That means making the CEO visible early and at key announcements throughout the process.
- **Stay on message.** Never make accidental news. Rigorously brief key officials prior to any announcement and role-play all awkward questions to ensure consistency of messages.
- **Demonstrate caring** about people. Recognize public anxiety, don't dismiss it.

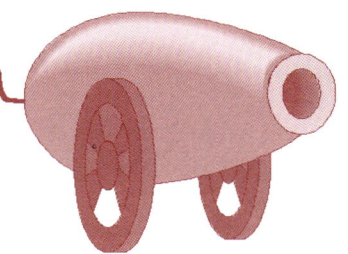

6 Crisis Concepts

1. Make Communications a Priority

- anticipate and lead, not merely react;
- be visible, not hidden;
- be organized and coherent;
- be responsive to the media's requirements;
- be clearly in the driver's seat of communications, and
- avoid making communications itself the issue.

2. A Crisis Occurs with Little or No Warning

- Afterwards, it is often discovered that early warning signals may have been discounted or ignored.
- There are significant areas for potential miscommunications - in understanding, contacting individuals and feeding accurately into and from the organization's center.

3. Don't Rely Solely on the Media

The media play a significant role in a crisis; but they are not the only players.
- Clear, direct channels of communications with other organizations and agencies, stakeholders, communities are vital to success.

4. It is Easy to Manage the Wrong Issue

- Uncover the real issue which can be obscured or can remain hidden.
- The media often determine the issue. It is vital to look at the issue from the perspective of the media (or high profile or "credible" group) as that's how the issue will be framed for the public.
- Set clear objectives in order to restore order or return quickly to 'normal'.

5. The Media Can Help or Hinder Your Response

- They are often the first to find out, even before you do.
- They report early and constantly.
- They can get your message out.
- They can warn the public.
- Can obscure facts - especially if you do a poor job communicating what you know.
- They decide early on in the crisis who is credible and who isn't.
- If you try to shut them out, they'll seek other sources - without the benefit of your perspective.
- Your goals are to be honest, accessible, responsive and visible.

6. If You Wait Until You Know Everything to Communicate, You'll Never Say Anything

- A great deal of time in a crisis is spent trying to discover facts and sort out confusion.
- Stand-by tools can allow you to 'hit the ground running' with accurate information and coherent direction.

10 Principles of Effective Crisis Communications

1. **In a Crisis, Issues Mutate**
   - Once one issue emerges, another one will pop up.
   - Don't get caught dealing solely with yesterday's issue.
   - Anticipate the natural flow of issues as well as "what if" scenarios.
   - Be seen to act immediately.

2. **Designate a Single Spokesperson - "Many Brains, One Mouth"** Concept

3. **Communicate Early and Often**
   - The first few hours present an ideal opportunity to shape the image of the organization and to influence media coverage and public perception.
   - Communicating early shows you have nothing to hide, and are straight-forward.
   - Use prepared tools such as backgrounders, initial statement, fact sheets, etc. to get the information out even before you know everything.
   - Communicating often avoids the information vacuum which the media may try to fill with minor, irrelevant yet possibly juicy items which will keep the story in the news.
   - Communicating often also makes you, rather than others, a credible source for information.

© 1996 *McLoughlin MultiMedia Publishing Ltd.*

4. **Encourage the 'Front Door' Approach**
   Welcome the media to your front door so that they won't try a side window or the back door (ex-employees, unnamed accusers, etc.).

5. **Get Ahead of the Curve**
   Anticipate all bad news incidents or allegations and prepare media tools such as backgrounders, fact sheets, etc., so you will be in communicating mode even before there is much to say.

6. **If There is Bad News Ahead, You Announce It**
   - If the media or another party reveals bad news, you will be perceived as trying to hide it.
   - Be the accurate source of verifiable facts.

7. **Get All the Bad News Out at Once - Have a Bad News Day - Not a Month**
   If there are a number of embarrassments to come in the story, real or perceived, announce them all at once. This will give you a bad day, rather than a bad month.

8. **Don't "Break into Jail"***
   If you are not the focus point of a crisis, don't make yourself one by:
   - drawing fire yourself with unguarded comments or perplexing actions;
   - being pro-active for the sake of it, and

   Remember that reporters covering a wounded person or organization ultimately enjoy the blood sport and the bleeding will go on until there is no more blood left or another, more significant victim trips and falls.

9. **"Quit While You're Behind"***
   If you're obviously losing the card game and everything you say is being undervalued, then fold your hand and come back another day when time has healed the wounds and new perspectives have been developed.

10. **Mop Up After the Mess**
    Conduct a post-mortem - not to hunt down the guilty, but to learn from what happened and apply the lessons next time.

* *These two principles are courtesy of Joseph T. Whelan, Whelan Communications, Chicago, Illinois.*

Crisis Communications Plan

Background Planning → **Establish Goals** (1) → **Potential Crises Assessment** (2) → **Audience Analysis** (3)

1. Overall Goals

- Control the flow of information.
- Establish the spokesperson/media center as the source of information about the incident/issue.
- Maintain perspective.
- Limit the news story to 24 hours.
- Contain the story to the local news if possible.

Crisis Management - Phase I
(as crisis begins)

- facilitate rapid de-escalation of the immediate crisis
- restore public order
- return to normal operations

Crisis Management - Phase II
(crisis under way)

- position organization as capable of managing the actual incident, event or allegation which has triggered the crisis in the first place
- ensure that all decisions and public statement are made from a common, up-to-date base of information
- eliminate errors via miscommunication through rapid dissemination of information
- prevent crisis escalation

Crisis Management - Phase III
(as crisis fades)

- rebuild, recover, re-establish public composure and repair relationships
- prevent recurrence or development of a chronic crisis
- enable the organization and its representatives to emerge with the highest possible credibility

© 1996 *McLoughlin MultiMedia Publishing Ltd.*

An effective crisis communications plan should:

- define response strategies that can be implemented when a crisis occurs;
- assign crisis communications resources and responsibilities;
- enable you to reach target audiences with key messages; and
- enable crisis communications managers to launch public information and media relations campaigns immediately during a crisis.

2. Potential Crises Assessment

Conduct regular scan of all possible crisis issues or events. Review crisis communications plan.

3. Audience Analysis

In a crisis, who really needs to know your messages?

Communications Personnel & Roles → **Initial Responders Communications Team 4** → **Crisis Communications Team 5** → **Spokesperson 6**

4. Initial Responders Communications Team

Local, site-specific communications or operational personnel. Trained to give a limited message and deal with initial media inquiries before the arrival of the Crisis Communications Team.

5. Crisis Communications Team

Identify key members, organize and train them, have available on a 24-hour basis, 7 days a week.

6. Spokesperson

Identify a single corporate spokesperson in addition to an on-site initial responder team with a limited communications role.

Crisis Communications Team

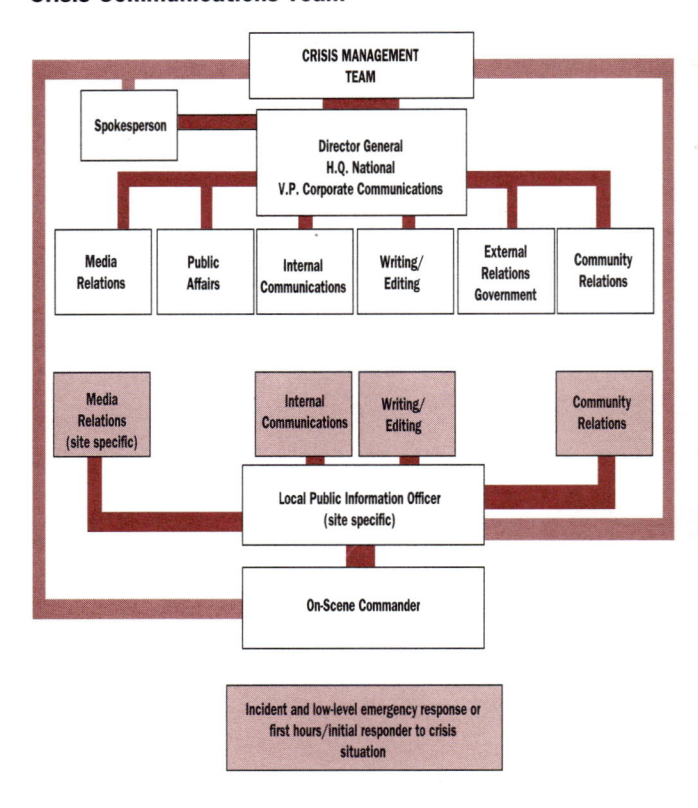

```
                    ┌─────────────────────┐
                    │  CRISIS MANAGEMENT  │
                    │        TEAM         │
                    └──────────┬──────────┘
                               │
   ┌──────────────┐  ┌─────────┴──────────────┐
   │ Spokesperson │──│   Director General     │
   └──────────────┘  │      H.Q. National     │
                     │ V.P. Corporate         │
                     │    Communications      │
                     └────────────┬───────────┘
```

| Media Relations | Public Affairs | Internal Communications | Writing/ Editing | External Relations Government | Community Relations |

| Media Relations (site specific) | | Internal Communications | Writing/ Editing | | Community Relations |

Local Public Information Officer (site specific)

On-Scene Commander

Incident and low-level emergency response or first hours/initial responder to crisis situation

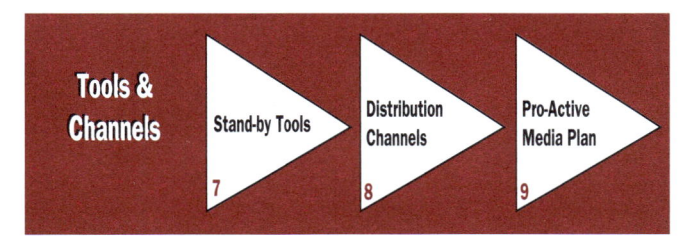

7. Stand-by Tools

Prepared range of stand-by, templated tools pre-authorized in substance for immediate public release. Includes: messages (have prepared messages for all potential crisis issues and events), announcements, fact sheets, backgrounders, advisories, news releases, press lines, audio and video modules, Internet and E-mail announcements, 1-800 systems, fax-broadcast and fax-on-demand capabilities, emergency channel announcements, etc.

8. Distribution Channels

Identify targeted and general distribution methods to reach your audiences.

9. Pro-Active Media Plan

- Establish a media monitoring system.
- Create a rapid response capability - who to call; when; how.

See the Media Relations tab of this booklet for further details.

10. Media Centers

Identify and prepare media centers near worksites, plants, etc. Ensure each has dedicated telephone lines and that portable radios and cell phones are available to establish communications in the event of telephone disruptions.

11. Equipment

- Ensure that adequate support equipment is available, and have it checked regularly. This includes word processors, video and cassette recorders, photocopiers and fax machines.
- Ensure that emergency power is available. Consider the installation of an emergency generator to ensure an adequate emergency power supply and clearly mark all outlets carrying this power supply.

Contacts & Activities: Call-Out List (12), Back-up & Administrative Staff (13), Partners/Allies (14), Communications Initiatives (15)

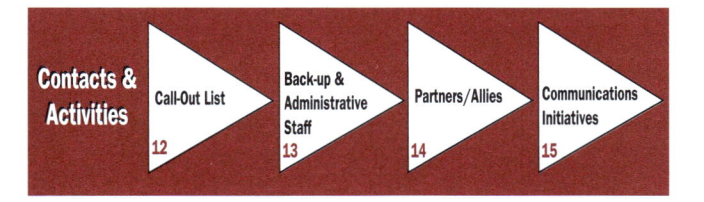

12. Call-Out List

Prepare a call-out list and update it regularly. This list should include everyone designated to respond in the event of a crisis, including the designated technical experts. Telephone numbers change often, which means this list should be checked and updated at least once a month. Also, ensure that a system is in place to notify these personnel in the event of telephone disruptions.

13. Back-up & Administrative Staff

Ensure that adequate back-up staff are available. If the crisis lasts more than 24 hours, it's a good idea to plan for replacement staff to come in and take over some of the support.

Before a crisis, support staff should ensure that equipment is maintained in good working order. During a crisis staff should provide logistical support in such areas as computers, telecommunications, and in answering incoming telephone calls.

14. Partners/Allies

Third-party allies/partners include: emergency response personnel (firefighters, police, etc.), government agencies, industry associations, environmental groups, community groups, health and safety officials. It is vital to form strong links with these third parties as they are often seen as more credible by the public and media.

15. Communications Initiatives

1) The First Two Hours
- Switch-on plan
- Agree on the lead agency
- Collect information
- Confirm facts
- Define the nature of a crisis
- Determine key actions
- Brief key spokesperson
- Prepare media tools

2) The First News Cycle
- Deploy crisis management team
- Stay ahead of events
- Listen and respond
- Remain calm

3) Respond to the Media
- Be quick - ensure that a brief statement is released as quickly as possible. If information is not yet available, or if you have just arrived, tell reporters you don't know yet what happened, you're about to be briefed, and you will be issuing a statement shortly. Then do it.
- Acknowledge responsibility as quickly as possible. If you've verified that responsibility for the crisis lies with your Organization, acknowledge this as quickly as possible to defuse negative media attention. But don't stop there. Continue by stressing what actions you're taking to address the problem. Never try to cover anything up. The media will find out and your credibility may be irreversibly damaged.
- Arrange for extra security. Extra security may be needed immediately outside your office complex to direct media personnel, and also within your building to escort reporters and others to and from the media center. If another location is involved, security may be needed there as well.
- Follow-up.
- Keep track of coverage: find out who used your story idea and how it came across.
- Conduct a media content analysis at periodic intervals to assess trend of stories.
- Develop new angles to freshen-up on-going issues.
- If you are creative in your thinking, you can make your story more attractive and marketable.
- Your task: demonstrate integrity, honesty and willingness to co-operate.
  It is inevitable that you will be subject to negative

attacks. Critical for your credibility is how you choose to respond to such attacks, if at all.
- If you do decide to respond, remember that your response must be cool, low-key and dignified.
- Keep the focus of your response on the facts and take the high road by refusing to resort to personal attacks or cheap shots.

4) Day Two
- Get help
- Reduce danger
- Obtain control
- Maintain media credibility

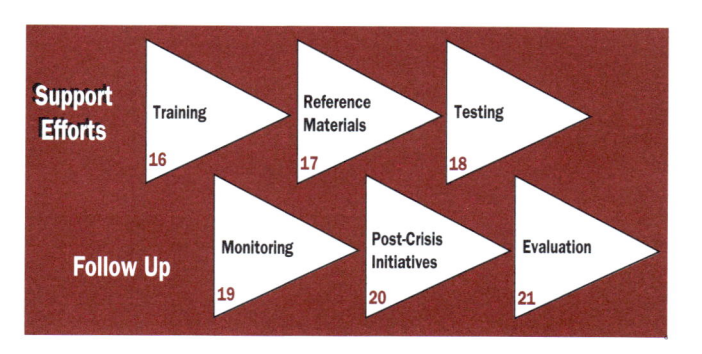

Support Efforts

16. Training

All personnel who are expected to communicate internally or externally in a crisis should be trained. Crisis Communications training should focus on building skills to:
- understand and assess risk;
- communicate with stakeholders directly and through the media;
- handle difficult questions, and
- develop crisis communications plans and tools.

17. Reference Materials

- Annual reports, environmental and safety reports, publicly available financial information.
- Chemicals list - all elements used on-site with toxicity levels, etc.
- Safety and emergency response plans and procedures.
- Safety record; environmental incidents and records.
- Operational details.
- Maps and charts.
- Facility and employee data.
- Product list.

18. Testing

All crisis communications plans and skills should be tested periodically. Either prepared or spontaneous simulations. Include external representatives - other agencies, media and community groups. Test not only the procedures, but the equipment and supplies to make sure they are readily available and in good working order.

Follow Up

19. Monitoring

It is vital for the crisis communications team to track and measure public and media reaction. It requires assigning personnel to:
- monitor all broadcast media;
- flag and review all pertinent media reports;
- track internet and web site comments and questions;
- track 1-800, e-mail and fax lines for trends in comments and questions, and
- engage in active listening program with community.

20. Post-Crisis Initiatives

After the crisis is over:
- issue a final news release to summarize what happened; what further steps will be taken or further information required;
- internal communications program to recognize special performance and to share learning;
- personal meetings and letters from the top executive to those who were affected by the situation, and
- thank you letters to partner agencies and those who helped in the response.

21. Evaluation

Once the crisis is brought under control, and the media spotlight has dimmed, conduct a review of the crisis communications response, including:
- public opinion - survey public attitudes;
- survey employees to determine their reactions and suggestions for improvement, and
- invite feedback from partner-agencies and third parties.

Remember:
- Adopt a "front door" approach
- Rapid response capability needed
- Pre-approved media materials
- Show concern
- Reassure
- Keep a record of event
- Don't speculate
- Be concise
- Control tone
- Change plan as required

Media Relations

- *overall media relations*
- *risk consultations and the media*
- *initial responders and the media*
- *crises and the media*

Overall Media Relations

Know Your Media

There are many variables which determine the media's coverage of an incident or issue:

- **Media Agenda:** If the incident occurs on a slow news day, then it could attract significant coverage. So, if you've got embarrassing or bad news to announce, try to pick an extremely busy news day.
- **Profile of the Issue:** If a particular issue is seen as a "front burner" agenda item then the issue is more attractive to the media. Issues which are always high profile include: sex, hypocrisy, illicit activities, political interference, AIDS, bureaucratic incompetence, etc.
- **Resources:** If the location of the incident, or the complexity of the issue requires too many resources for the media to be able to cover it, then chances are it won't receive much play.

- **Fits the Definition of News:** That which is unusual, unexpected, of wide significance, generates "heat" or public outrage, involves a public figure, money or damage, is judged to be blatantly stupid or lacking in common sense, symbolic or symptomatic of a significant issue or growing trend.
- **Has Visuals or Audio to Support it:** What is news to television may not be news to print or radio. Access to visuals or audio clips will spell the difference for coverage by the broadcast media.

Keys to Effective Media Relations

- **Work with the media.** The media will go to whomever they want for comments anyway. If you develop a coherent approach and appropriate media tools, and present an organized image, the media will quickly see that their needs can be met through cooperation, rather than confrontation.

- **Develop a coherent strategy.** Random coverage just for the sake of exposure rarely does any good. A focused, strategic media approach creates a sense of control and calm in what otherwise could prove to be a panic-inducing atmosphere the moment a negative story comes out. You want the communication team to focus their energies on the work at hand. Developing a healthy, productive media relationship with a strategic vision can go a long way toward creating a calm, productive atmosphere.

- **Begin by collecting basic information** on who's who in the media:
  - Media outlets
  - Reporters and editors
  - Issues/topics

It is vital to develop effective working relationships with the media before controversies arise. There is no reason why your relationship with the media has to be adversarial. Indeed, your goal should be to work with the media; not so much to "educate" the media but to build mutual respect and understanding.

Several Cautions About Media Relations

- **The media are not your mouthpieces.** The decision to cover the issue or event will be made in individual newsrooms by editors and producers.
- **The media hate any attempts to manipulate them.** You should not cajole, berate or otherwise try to make the media do anything. Instead, the media respond to what they consider to be the "news value" or relevance of your issues to their audiences. Managing media relations is a bit like attempting to push a snake up a hill. In other words, the media don't always go where you want them to and they take their own time about doing it. As well, they can always turn around and bite the "handler"! So don't try to manage the media, so much as manage the relationship between your organization and the media. Ideally, it should be a win-win relationship in which both parties get something out of it.
- **The media look for an angle.** They approach the issue from a certain perspective which they believe is newsworthy or relevant, usually with some aspect of controversy attached to it. Sometimes, it can completely surprise you. The angle can often be driven by critics of the organization. Make sure that you clearly understand the angle on which the media are focusing so that you can be prepared for the media coverage.

- **Process can cancel out content.** What led to the issue's relevance may well be more interesting to the media than the substance of the issue. If the people involved in the issue are controversial then the media can become focused on the personalities rather than the issue. So, choose your team members carefully.
- **Don't confuse being "friendly" with being "friends".** A good healthy relationship with the media does not mean compromising a story because of a personal "friendship". Do not place a reporter in a compromised situation. Building trust with a reporter is founded on a healthy respect for your very different roles and obligations.

Tactics for Dealing With the Media

What to do if the Story is Wrong

- If a story is inaccurate, don't over-react. Call the reporter or the editor or producer, and politely point out the error. If it's significant, ask for an immediate correction in the next edition or report. If not satisfied, call the managing editor or the executive producer and fax in a "request for correction", supporting it with evidence.
- Almost all newspapers are "on line" in a computer database. Any corrections made to the story will be flagged for future reference in follow-up stories so that inaccuracies are not repeated.
- If the story has an unfair, derisive tone to it which, in your view, is undeserved, write a letter to the editor or executive producer that coolly lays out your response. You might get a better shake on the next story. Don't be offensive or whining in tone.
- If you don't like the story, but it is factually based, you're better to leave it alone.
- If it's a real hatchet job based on inaccuracies and innuendo by an influential media outlet, issue a press release to other media correcting the facts or take out an ad in that newspaper.
- If it's a television or radio program that is inaccurate, ask the producer if you can be interviewed to refute the charges or to have your reaction comments included in the next program.

- Legal action is difficult to win, but is a last resort if the story is fundamentally inaccurate, malicious and damaging. Don't threaten legal action unless you mean it. Stay cool and let your lawyer handle it.
- If it's a minor media outlet or a discredited tabloid paper or program, don't draw unnecessary attention to it unless mainstream media pick up the story.
- If it's not serious, let it go and save your ammunition for when it counts.

For preventive medicine, tell the reporter that you would like to record the interview "so that I can have a record of it." It signals the reporter not to play fast and loose with the editing because you will have a transcript.

What to do if the Story is Right

Be cautious about "thanking" a reporter for a story which made you look good. If you do express thanks, don't do so in front of other reporters. Instead, praise the reporter for writing a 'fair and balanced' story.

Questions to Ask the Reporter on Initial Contact

If a reporter calls to inform you of an incident or a rapidly evolving story and you are caught unaware, try to be as helpful as possible; but don't automatically agree to be interviewed until you know more about the incident.

Ask **some** of the following questions:
1. Your name again?
2. Representing what media outlet?
3. What is it about?
4. Can you give me any specifics?
5. How much do you know about our organization (or the subject)?
6. May I call you back as soon as I can confirm something?
7. What is your deadline?
8. In the meantime, I can FAX some background information to you. Your FAX number? Your phone number?

Call back when you promised, even if it's to reassure the reporter that you're still trying to clarify the situation.

Interview Ground Rules

Be prepared to live with everything you say to a reporter or you shouldn't say it at all. Occasionally, however, the issue of ground rules may arise.

On-the-record: Everything you say can be quoted and you can be named (the way it is unless otherwise negotiated in advance).

Off-the-record: The reporter agrees to take information from a protected source without writing a story or using the information in any way. This, however, does not prevent the reporter from getting the same information from another source and using it. **Not advisable!**

For background or not-for-attribution: The reporter can use the information with direct quotes but not name the source: e.g. "A senior official close to the investigation who asked not to be identified said, 'this problem has been bubbling below the surface...'"

Deep background or guidance: A protected source who can't be identified or directly quoted, but the information can be used to guide the reporter in the direction of the story: e.g. "It is well-known within the Department that this situation..."

Tips for Dealing with Journalists

1. Respect their deadlines. Return their calls.
2. Be polite. Never lose your temper.
3. Try to be helpful.
4. If you don't know the answer, say so, but offer to find it.
5. Always tell the truth. Don't lie or be evasive.
6. Don't say "no comment". It is often interpreted as "it's true, but I just can't admit it."
7. Stick to your area of responsibility. Don't speak on behalf of others.
8. Anticipate reporters' needs. Prepare and update fact sheets and talking points constantly.
9. Don't create a vacuum. Journalists have to report! If you don't feed them, someone else will!
10. Treat reporters like human beings. Give a little (cooperation); get a little in return.
11. Avoid coming across as "thin skinned," i.e. overly sensitive about negative stories. Keep your perspective.

© 1996 McLoughlin MultiMedia Publishing Ltd.

Risk and Crisis Media Tips

1. **Be Pro-Active:** Anticipate, do your homework, study the history of the issue, region, key players, media coverage, etc. However, don't be pro-active just for the sake of it.

2. **Reach Out:** Contact opinion leaders and credible third-party advocates who can make your case for you.

3. **Respond Rapidly:** Don't let attacks which appear to have credibility go unchallenged. If it's a negative story which only touches on your organization, don't turn up the heat on yourself by entering the fray.

4. **Frame the Issue(s):** Be the first to frame the issue or others will do it for you. e.g. "The issue is, whose side is the government on?"

5. **Manage the Tone:** Avoid sounding arrogant and avoid tactics such as treating opponents with contempt, or questioning their motives. The ideal is "more in sadness than in anger."

6. **Adopt a Front-Door Approach:** Open the front door for the media, or they'll find the side window or back door and "get the story" anyway. If you tell reporters to go away, they may find a more comfortable home to welcome them... which may pose great discomfort for you.

7. **Admit Mistakes:** If you make a mistake, admit it immediately and make the issue what you're doing to ensure it doesn't happen again.

8. **Communicate Internally:** First, if you're making a major announcement, make sure you tell your employees and partner agencies' employees before they hear about it from the media.

9. **Be First With Any Bad News:** Be the first to announce the bad news and get all of it out at once. Avoid the media feeding frenzy which will develop if they discover it first.

10. **Communicate Early and Often:** The moment something happens, get in the driver's seat with the media by communicating quickly, accurately and often.

Risk Consultations and the Media

If you are planning to involve the public in a consultation process, it is vital to consider the media in your planning. Overwhelmingly, the public will receive its information about the subject, your attempts at involving the public and the outcome of the process through television, radio and newspaper accounts - if they hear about it at all.

Without media coverage, your public consultation process will be very much like the proverbial tree falling in the middle of the forest. Did it make a sound?

Involving the media is a delicate operation at best. You should not be in the business of trying to manipulate the media. Leaving aside the ethical issues, in the end a manipulated media will become your worst enemy.

Establish Your Media Relations Goals for a Consultation

What are your goals when it comes to involving media in a public consultation on a risk issue?

Goals

- to get the messages out as to the objectives of the consultation, the type of input the panel, commission or task force is seeking, and the stakes attached to the issues being examined.
- to convey critical information about the locations and times of public hearings, objective facts surrounding the issues and the context in which the issues fit.
- to get the attention of the public so that the public can see the relevance of the issues to their lives.
- to focus on building understanding, that is "shedding light" instead of "adding heat" or creating fear and anxiety
- to avoid public displays of disunity among the panel members
- to make deliberate news, not accidental news

Accidental news usually means fear or allegation-driven stories which generate increased anxiety, decreased trust in the process and the consulting agency caught up in fire-fighting.

Remember, however, that the media's goals are different from yours. The media will look for what is new, - not because it is necessarily important in the overall scheme of things, but because it might be interesting, unexpected, controversial - in other words - "news"!!!

Media's Stake in Consultation Process

- voice of the people
- reflect criticisms/concerns
- frame the issue in understandable terms
- surface the real agenda
- focus on substance and process or conflict
- concerned about their own credibility

The Media's Ability to Create and Drive the Process

The media…
- create expectations
- set performance expectations
- benchmark performance standards
- hold officials, agencies and companies accountable
- provide forum for supporters and critics
- capture emotions and attitudes
- create a forum for controversy
- contrast opinions

Controlling the Communications Process

- develop a media relations strategy
- organize how and when media information is provided
- decide on a spokesperson
- 'hit the ground running' so that your organization is not immobilized
- work to 'stay ahead of the curve' in the provision of information

Getting Ahead of the Information Curve

Coverage is on-going and constant, therefore:
- the media have a need to 'freshen up' a story
- if you don't feed the media appetite, they'll look any morsel they can feed on
- have up-to-the minute information on media coverage in selected media outlets and in key markets
- develop media tools in advance*
  - backgrounders
  - fact sheets
  - questions and answers
  - media response lines
  - interview plan sheets

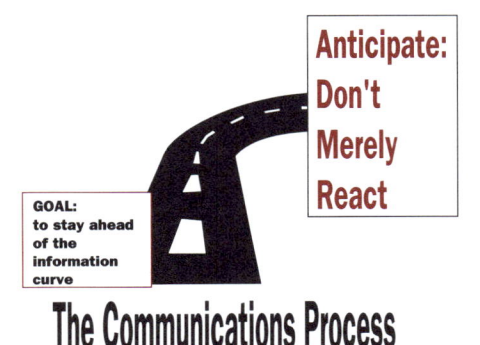

Anticipate: Don't Merely React

GOAL: to stay ahead of the information curve

The Communications Process

see the Encountering the Media® pocket tips booklet

© 1996 McLoughlin MultiMedia Publishing Ltd.

Conducting a Consultation Process in The Media Spotlight

Once focused on a risk issue, the media hone in with a high-intensity spotlight. In effect, the media have the power to say "pay attention to this issue". Suddenly, a risk issue can become heated overnight.

The inner circle (1) attracts the laser beam of the media spotlight through high-profile consultation initiatives such as referenda, hearings, or major media tours and through support tools such as advertising. The middle circle (2) includes event-specific media coverage such as stakeholder meetings, speeches, etc. The outer circle (3) of consulting is just on the fringe of the media spotlight and tends to attract targeted media and industry publicity, and includes community liaison groups and information letters.

Communicate With Power Risk Consultation Modeller™

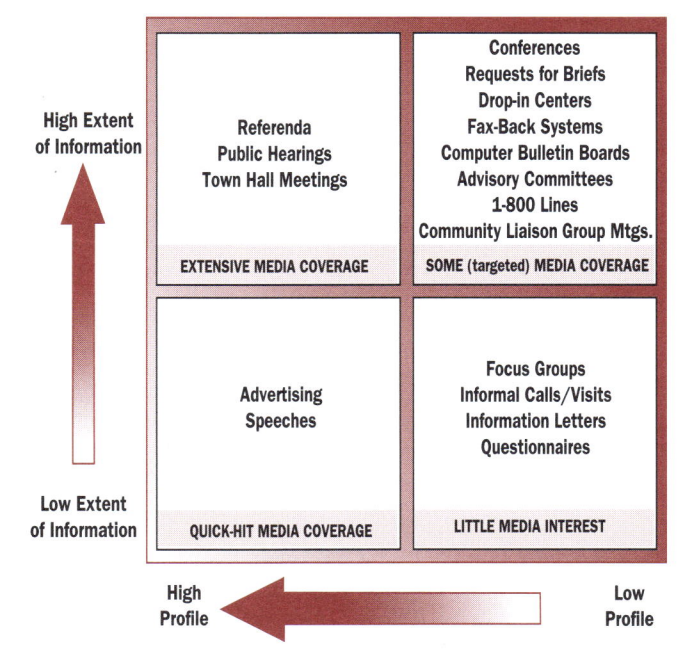

	High Profile	Low Profile
High Extent of Information	Referenda Public Hearings Town Hall Meetings *EXTENSIVE MEDIA COVERAGE*	Conferences Requests for Briefs Drop-in Centers Fax-Back Systems Computer Bulletin Boards Advisory Committees 1-800 Lines Community Liaison Group Mtgs. *SOME (targeted) MEDIA COVERAGE*
Low Extent of Information	Advertising Speeches *QUICK-HIT MEDIA COVERAGE*	Focus Groups Informal Calls/Visits Information Letters Questionnaires *LITTLE MEDIA INTEREST*

© 1996 McLoughlin MultiMedia Publishing Ltd.

Whetting the Media's Appetite in a Consultation Process

First, you have to create the appetite. Whetting the appetite means:

- **Defining the problems or issues which your task force, commission or panel of experts will be exploring.** Can you state the issue simply? Does it have meaning or relevance to the public? Why should we care about this issue? What's in it for us to either know more about this issue or to have a solution to the problem? That is known as "relating the issue".
- **Deciding on your messages.** You want the public and the media to know what the objectives of the consultations are. Thus, there should be a set of coherent, simple messages aimed at the publics with whom you would like to engage in a dialogue. They should be readily understandable and should be threaded throughout all publications and interviews as well as in public hearings so that over time, they begin to sink in.
- **Illustrating the problems or issues.** We live in a "post-literate" society to a great extent. In other words, the public no longer has to read in order to "be informed". Therefore, if we can't see it on our television screens we don't really know about it. When you combine this with the massive "information overload" experienced by everybody in our society you are competing with every other issue in the rapidly shrinking attention span of the public.

- **Targeting and prioritizing your audiences.** Don't think of the public as one large amorphous mass. If you do that you won't be able to relate to anyone. Segment your marketplace - demographically. List them according to the importance of these issues to their lives. Segment audiences according to their *importance vs. urgency.* That is, don't just give them priority because they are the "squeakiest wheel".
- **Targeting your media.** Know who the key media players are, who they represent and what they are interested in.

Crises and the Media

What the Media Do In a Crisis

- find out about crisis
  - very quickly
  - often before you do
- monitor each other/emergency communications channels
- divert extra resources and personnel to cover crisis
- allot extra time and space for coverage of crisis
- go to the site
  - before you do
  - in large numbers
- go where they want, unless clear boundaries have been set up
- tie up your telephone lines and personnel
- probe for details
- demanding
- share information
- use sophisticated equipment
- use their own knowledge, experience and archives
- report what they know - quickly, constantly and endlessly
- lay blame
- perpetuate myths
- report rumors

What the Media Can Do For You

- assist in pre-crisis education
- warn
- reinforce a warning
- get your requests to the public
- get information to the public
- get information to a specific segment of the public
- get your point of view to the public
- reassure the public
- repudiate rumors
- help the response
- be a source of information for you
- generate outside help

The Most Asked Media Questions in a Crisis - Are You Prepared to Answer Them?

- What happened?
- When and where?
- Who was involved?
- Why? What was the cause?
- What are you going to do about it?
- How much damage?
- What safety measures were taken?
- Who's to blame?
- Do you accept responsibility? liability?
- Has this ever happened before?
- What do you have to say to the victims?
- How does this affect your operations?
- Any witnesses? Can we speak to them?

Initial Responders and the Media

The media are often already on-site when the initial responders arrive. Until the incident or event is clarified, any communications must be limited. However, some key information must be communicated before the spokespoerson arrives, in order to avoid public panic or misinformation.

Initial Responders' Media Messages

If confronted by the media at the outset of the event, a trained initial responder should limit his or her comments to the following:
- "We have just arrived on-site.
- Our immediate concern is to secure the area, ensure that the employees and the public, are safe...
- Our goal is to contain the spill, limit the spread, etc.
- We are asking for your cooperation to stay back in order to ensure public safety (or the safety of those inside).
- We will keep you posted as soon as we have more information.
- We cannot confirm the cause… the amount of damage etc.
- We do not intend to speculate.
- For all other questions I would refer you to our public affairs personnel who will be arriving shortly."

The Initial Public Statement (Positioning Statement)

Within minutes of an event or allegation, make every effort to release a public statement which gives the basic information on the incident or issue. Follow up later with a more detailed statement. Include:
- What happened?
- Where did it happen?
- When?
- How many people were injured? killed? involved?
- What you are doing to deal with it (emergency plan).
- Include brief, key information on the site involved, the chemicals or products and the company.
- How and when further information can be made available.
- Be clear in your positioning of the issue: are you
  a) flatly denying the charge?
  b) in agreement?
  c) investigating? looking into the allegation?
  d) cooperating fully with officials?

Do not speculate on...

- the amount of damage
- the costs to the company
- the cause
- the condition of personnel
- the implications of the allegation or incident

Remember...

- Withhold names of injured or deceased until next-of-kin have been properly notified
- Acknowledge responsibility, but avoid prematurely laying blame at anyone's doorstep.

Develop a Media Strategy

A media strategy can be utilized to support risk, communications, emergency or crisis communications efforts.

Definition

Media Strategy

A means to achieve a specific public relations or communications goal through an organized earned media campaign.

Why have a Media Strategy?

- To support the organization's overall mission statement and communications strategy.
- To manage issues which should be covered by the media or dealt with effectively in the media.
- To ensure that media relations does not become an issue of concern.
- To allow the organization to respond to and generate media coverage as desired.
- To avoid a purely reactive approach which usually ends 'puuting out fires' instead of being pro-active.

A Media Strategy Will…

- Define issues in the environment surrounding the organization which may impact upon it.
- Define the key stakeholders (relevant publics).
- Identify the needs, concerns and issues of those stakeholders.
- Articulate core messages which drive the organization's media communications.
- Outline a program to inform and initiate action.
- Define specific outcomes for the program.
- Identify how other communications initiatives relate to the media strategy.
- Describe how the strategy can be objectively evaluated.

Be Pro-Active

Being pro-active means a planned effort to initiate media interest in a subject or issue. Most often the effort is to generate a "feature" or a "soft news" story targeted at a section of the newspaper, or a television or radio news magazine program.

The Framework for a Media Strategy

Encountering the Media **Issues Planner**™	1. Document Title
▶ 2. Issue Description	
▶ 3. Media Analysis	▶ 10. Issue Management Team
▶ 4. Issue Analysis	▶ 11. Spokespersons
▶ 5. Issue Management Goals	▶ 12. Messages, themes, etc.
▶ 6. Strategy	▶ 13. Fact Gathering Requirements
▶ 7. Target Audiences	▶ 14. Media Tools & Activities
▶ 8. Stakeholders	▶ 15. Action Plan
▶ 9. Media Targets	▶ 16. Budget

See the Encountering the Media® Pocket Tips Booklet or software ToolKit® for detailed instructions to complete a media strategy.

The Media Strategy

1) Give the strategy a title.
2) Describe the issue.
3) Analyze the media coverage to date.
4) Analyze how the issue is being portrayed by critics, politicians, etc.
5) State the goals in the management of the issue and how the goals will be evaluated.
6) Capture the overall essence of the strategy.
7) Target your audiences and rank them accordingly.
8) Identify the stakeholders in the issue.
9) Target which media need to be reached and how.
10) Identify the communications team members.
11) Identify the spokespersons - site locations, HQ etc.
12) State the messages and themes.
13) Outline the facts to be gathered.
14) Describe the media tools and initiatives to be undertaken.
15) Set out the action plan to implement - with timetables and include a monitoring and evaluation component.
16) Outline the budget for the strategy, including personnel.

Supporting Components of a Media Strategy

Pro-Active Media Opportunities

- **Appearance on talk shows:** reaches a large audience, requires hook with broad appeal.
- **Backgrounder:** background briefing for selected reporters, usually held in conjunction with major announcement or event. Also a one or two page note which provides context, background, chronology, explanation to support an announcement, interview, news conference, etc.
- **Editorial board meeting:** provides in-depth background to newspaper editors, on-the-record.
- **Information-for-file:** one or two pages with covering note, provided periodically to targeted journalists for background information.
- **Letter-to-the-editor and guest editorial:** opportunity to present comments in your words.
- **Media advisory:** a "heads up" to media on the wire to draw attention to up-coming event.
- **Media availability session or media briefing:** less formal than a news conference; news maker is available for interviews at an event (e.g. speech, opening, etc.).
- **Media interview:** one-on-one or with another guest or two; live or taped and edited; in person, on the telephone or via satellite; on-the-record.
- **Media tour:** media are invited to tour a work site, inspect a new facility or test out a new technology.
- **News articles:** prepared for community weeklies to provide greater detail.

- **News conference:** used only to communicate new and important messages.
- **News release:** objective is to draw attention to a significant development. Much over-used; should be utilized sparingly and only when there is a real news story, a new product or innovative service launched.
- **Teleconference:** the news maker is interviewed by a handful of reporters from different cities.

Media Support Tools

- **Information-for-file:** a targeted information tool sent to targeted reporters who have covered similar issues. One or two pages of updated information on the risk issue.
- **Media interview plan:** succinct summary of what to focus on during the interview. (See the Encountering the Media® Pocket Tips Booklet.)
- **Media response lines:** used to inject some discipline into the organization's interviews and public utterances. Gives key personnel some interesting and useful points to get across when speaking with journalists. Anticipates and helps prepare for awkward areas that could attract journalists' interest.
- **Questions and answers:** brainstorm all of the possible difficult questions your spokesperson may be asked and ensure that the team agrees on the answers.

Communications Roles in a Crisis

The Media Guide

The person assigned to stay in constant media contact. The Media Guide is a facilitator, not a spokesperson.

Roles

- **Monitor the media for errors.** This means watching, listening to and reading media reports. Inform the spokesperson of any errors.
- **Note the name and telephone numbers** of each reporter as well as the name and location of his/her station, publication or company. If the media do report errors or rumors, this list helps in getting a quick correction or clarification.
- **Take requests for information and comments.** By finding out what kinds of information the media want and who they want statements from, the media guide can get the information to address these needs directly.
- **Provide the media with logistical support.** Ensure that enough telephones and other support functions such as photocopying, food and beverages are available for media use and consumption.
- **Ask the reporters what kinds of information they are receiving.** Collecting and disseminating information is what a reporter's job is all about, which means the media are a good source of information for you. And, because the media guide never releases information, it is easier to move among the reporters, chatting and asking for information.

- **Establish regular contact and coordination of information between:**
  - Yourself and other spokespersons within your organization
  - Spokespersons from other organizations

  In this way information is shared and problems such as the release of conflicting or potentially damaging information can be avoided.
- **Ensure that information is shared with your organization's other offices.** Internal communication is important. This can be easily accomplished by fax machine or conference calls. Be sure to specify what information has been released.
- **Correct any errors or rumors as quickly as possible.**
- **Consider holding joint news conferences with other organizations.** Logistically, this may make life easier for all concerned, and it portrays a co-operative spirit of response.
- **Identify where visuals can be obtained.** Suggest locations media personnel can videotape and photograph, or from where they can obtain relevant visual material.
- **If a site is involved have it videotaped and provide these visuals to the media and those working in the operations room.** At times, for safety and other reasons, it may not be possible to give media personnel site access. In this type of situation have the site videotaped and provide this material to the media. Those working in isolation in the operations center will also find this material helpful as it gives them a

visual understanding of the situation.
- **Consider a guided media tour.** Determine what ground rules the media must follow, then take them on a tour of the affected area (if relevant) or other restricted areas, such as the operations center. Indicate clearly that if anyone breaks any of the rules the tour will be ended for all.
- **Make pool arrangements.** Another option is to arrange a media pool. You cannot manage a large group of media personnel at a sensitive site. You can, however, manage a group of up to 5 or 6 journalists. Approach the journalists and announce that a pool of reporters will be escorted to a location. Pick a number of categories (one print reporter, one radio reporter, one camera operator, etc.) and let the group fill the designated categories amongst themselves. They will choose colleagues with the most experience or best reputations for it is in their interest to get the best material. Those chosen for the pool are then escorted on condition they share all gathered material with those left behind.
- **Ensure that all released information is written in news release format.** In this way information can be easily shared with other involved players, such as those answering queries by telephone or fax, to other offices and other organizations.
- **Clearly number and post all news releases (with date and time).** Since not all reporters will be present for the initial briefings, late arrivals can simply consult the posted releases for any missed information, freeing other personnel from the task of updating new arrivals.

- **Never release information without allowing reporters to ask questions.** Reporters may simply not understand what you are trying to say, in which case your message will be lost, or worse still, misinterpreted and inaccurately reported. If you cannot answer a question, say so and explain why. If information is not yet available, explain that you will try to find the answers in time for the next briefing.
- **Provide visuals.** Remember that television and print reporters and photographers need visuals. Television reporters in particular cannot report what you are saying unless they have visuals to support your message. Graphics and photographs add credibility and accuracy to print coverage.
- **Hold frequent news conferences.** This is particularly important during the first 24 hours when media attention is most concentrated but information only trickles in. Announce and post the scheduled time of each conference, and never start before the announced time.
- **Record all briefings, conferences and interviews.** This gives you a record of what was released.
- **Arrange for others to make statements.** Other key officers, technical experts and on site managers may be called to attend news conferences. They can be introduced and made available at the news conference to respond to technical questions as required. This allows speakers to return to their primary functions after an appropriate time. The media guide can indicate which officials are of interest to reporters.

- **Release the prepared background material on those making statements.** This gives reporters an understanding of the role these persons play within the organization and takes care of such details as correct titles and spelling of names.
- **Release the public and media enquiry telephone numbers and the location of your media center.** The best way to publicize this information is to contact the media wire services. There are a number of commercial companies who can fax your release to whatever media you designate.
- **Ensure that staff are in place to answer and monitor these calls.** These persons can relay the public and media requests for information to the spokesperson and provide information already released to those calling in. In this way the spokesperson is informed of, and can get answers to, the specific questions and concerns of the general public and the media, and respond to them in press releases, briefings and conferences.
- **Release the prepared material.** This covers the initial period when very little information is available, which allows you to concentrate on gathering current data. The media will have a great void to fill, and will therefore be more inclined to report what you have to offer.

- **Arrange for a full news conference as quickly as possible.** Even if very little information is available, the conference gives broadcast media sound bites and visuals, and quotes to the written press. An early conference shows that you are organized not only in your press relations, but also in your response. It also establishes a routine with the media, and keeps them physically at one location – the media center.
- **Remember: Information is Power.** If you do not provide information the media will simply go to other sources and you will lose control of what reporters are saying and how they are portraying you. Adopt a "front door" strategic approach. In effect, you're saying to the media "come in the front door and we can provide you with information that is timely and factual."

The Spokesperson

The person designated to speak on behalf of the organization - either the senior communications official or a senior executive or a subject specialist. The more significant the issue or event, the more senior the spokesperson. The CEO or Agency Head, or the On-Scene Commander are invaluable spokespersons when the stakes are high.

The Spokesperson's Focus

- **Stress the positive - what you are doing to clear the problem up.** Even if the responsibility for the crisis does not lie with your organization, stress the positive actions you are taking to address the public concerns.
- **Collect - Evaluate - Recommend - Decide - Release.** Collect information. Evaluate it for potential release. Recommend what information can or should be released. Decide what should be released, when and how. And then release the information to the media.
- **Remember that you're not talking to the media, you're talking to the public.** The media provide a powerful filter for information to people in your community and the public at large.

Media Support Services

To be handled by communications and administrative support personnel. Keep in mind that the media want to be assisted, not controlled.

- **Collect and manage the release of information.** Providing logistical support and ensuring that media needs are met makes it easier for members of the media to do their job. They will appreciate your efforts, and remember their experiences when preparing reports involving your organization after the crisis is over.
- **Open the media center.** Or ensure that the first person to arrive has access to keys that will open the center.
- **Keep a log.** Note and indicate the time of all events, requests and decisions. In the heat of response some requests may be forgotten, and once the crisis is over a log is invaluable for debriefing purposes and to pinpoint problems that can be corrected.
- **Clearly mark where the media center is and distribute the identification passes to incoming media personnel.** Post the prepared signs at all entrances that can be accessed by the media, and ensure that all incoming personnel are given identification passes.
- **Double check all information before releasing it.** In the heat of any crisis response, information is incomplete, contradictory and changes constantly. It is extremely important to verify and double check all information. Anything less would be irresponsible, and given the concentrated media attention, potentially damaging to not only your organization but to other organizations as well.

Media Center

A *media center* is a designated site from which the media can operate in covering the incident, emergency or crisis. It should be set up near the site with a room large enough to hold 50 persons. An additional room adjacent to it for holding news conferences would be ideal.

Media Center - Equipment & Supply Checklist

(again, identify available sources and where resources can be installed easily)
- ✓ A television and battery-powered radio
- ✓ At least 10 telephones or jacks available for notebook computers
- ✓ An adequate number of power outlets
- ✓ Bulletin boards, flip charts and markers
- ✓ A photocopier (if possible)
- ✓ Desks and chairs
- ✓ Food and beverages
- ✓ If necessary, space in smaller rooms for television editors and producers

Portable Media Center

A mini-media center right at the site if it is remote. Ensure that personnel and equipment are available to move quickly to an on-site or near-site location. Ensure that a communication link such as a cellular or satellite telephone is available for communication between the on-site and off-site communications personnel.

*News Conference Room**

- ✓ High ceilings to accommodate television lights
- ✓ A large table at the front of the room to hold microphones. A uni-mic system to plug the microphones into.
- ✓ An appropriate corporate or Agency backdrop behind the table
- ✓ Sufficient power source with back-up

* See details in the Encountering the Media® pocket tips booklet.

Planning Tools

Consultation is Key to Credibility

- Consulting Agency
  - Community
  - Special Interest Groups
  - External Consultants
  - Regulators
  - Government Agencies
  - Employees

Risk Management Decision Process

1. Initiation
2. Preliminary Analysis
3. Risk Estimation
4. Risk Evaluation
5. Risk Control and Financing
6. Action
7. Monitoring and Evaluation

Goals of a Risk Communications Strategy

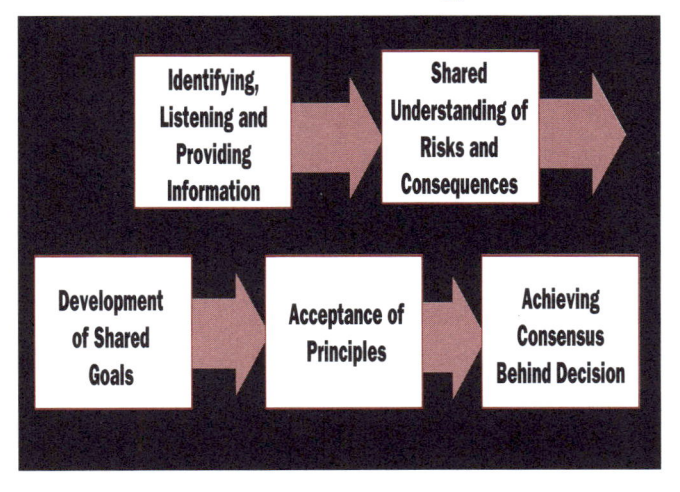

```
[Identifying, Listening and Providing Information] → [Shared Understanding of Risks and Consequences] →

[Development of Shared Goals] → [Acceptance of Principles] → [Achieving Consensus Behind Decision]
```

Communicate With Power Message Developer™

Tier One Steps

- **GOAL**: Define your goals.
- **AUDIENCE**: Define your primary target audiences
- **ISSUES**: Their concerns
- **NEED**: What do they need to know or be assured of?
- **PROACTIVE MESSAGES**: Prepare a set of four 'lead' messages

Tier Two Steps

- **THEME**: Develop a theme which pulls together your messages
- **REACTIVE MESSAGES**: Brought out if specifically asked
- **REFINE AND SIMPLIFY**: Cut jargon - "retail" the message to your audience's everyday realities
- **TEST**: Test your messages before delivering them (focus groups)

Tier Three Steps

- **POSITIONING STATEMENT**: Five or six sentences (30 seconds) to get started - could be background or summary of position on issue
- **EXAMPLES, ILLUSTRATIONS and QUOTABLE QUOTES**

© 1996 McLoughlin MultiMedia Publishing Ltd.

	Stakeholder 1	Stakeholder 2	Stakeholder 3
	Local community	Pulp & paper industry	Environmental groups
Why this stakeholder?	Potential impacts on environment & possible job loss	Economic stake	Environmental consequences
Risk perception focus	Concern about environmental impact	Concern that risk is being over-stated	Serious potential damage to air, water and fish habitat
Communications tools	Information kit Questionnaire Invitation	Backgrounder Invitation	Information kit Invitation
Consultation Models/Support Tools	Community Liaison Group (CLG) Kiosk at fair Meetings Letters Ads in Weeklies	Hearings Meetings	Hearings Meetings Letters
Responsibility	Risk Management team - Lead Communications - Support	Risk Management Team Communications - Coordinate	Scientific team - Lead Communications - Support
Time Frame	May-June	July-Sept.	July-Sept.
Message	We want your input	The process will be fair	We will follow all environmental regulations - your input is needed

Communicate With Power
Public Consultation Decision-Maker™

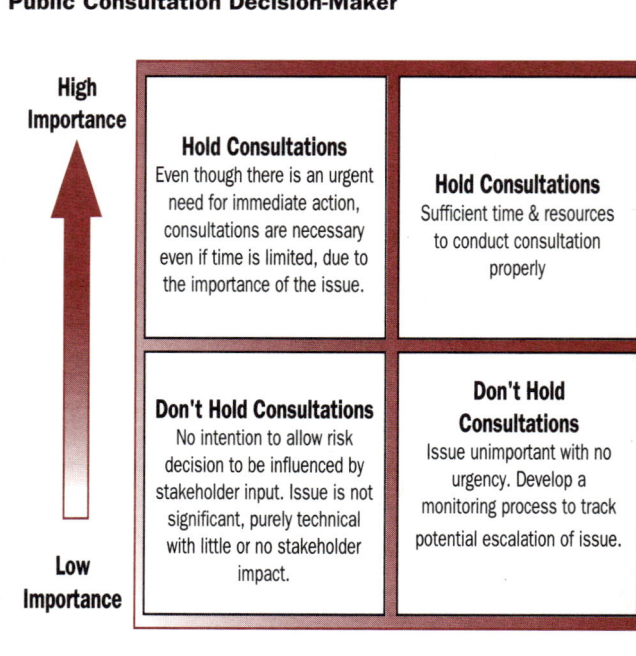

↑ High Importance / Low Importance

← High Urgency / Low Urgency

	High Urgency	Low Urgency
High Importance	**Hold Consultations** — Even though there is an urgent need for immediate action, consultations are necessary even if time is limited, due to the importance of the issue.	**Hold Consultations** — Sufficient time & resources to conduct consultation properly
Low Importance	**Don't Hold Consultations** — No intention to allow risk decision to be influenced by stakeholder input. Issue is not significant, purely technical with little or no stakeholder impact.	**Don't Hold Consultations** — Issue unimportant with no urgency. Develop a monitoring process to track potential escalation of issue.

© 1996 McLoughlin MultiMedia Publishing Ltd.

Communicate With Power Consultation Loop™

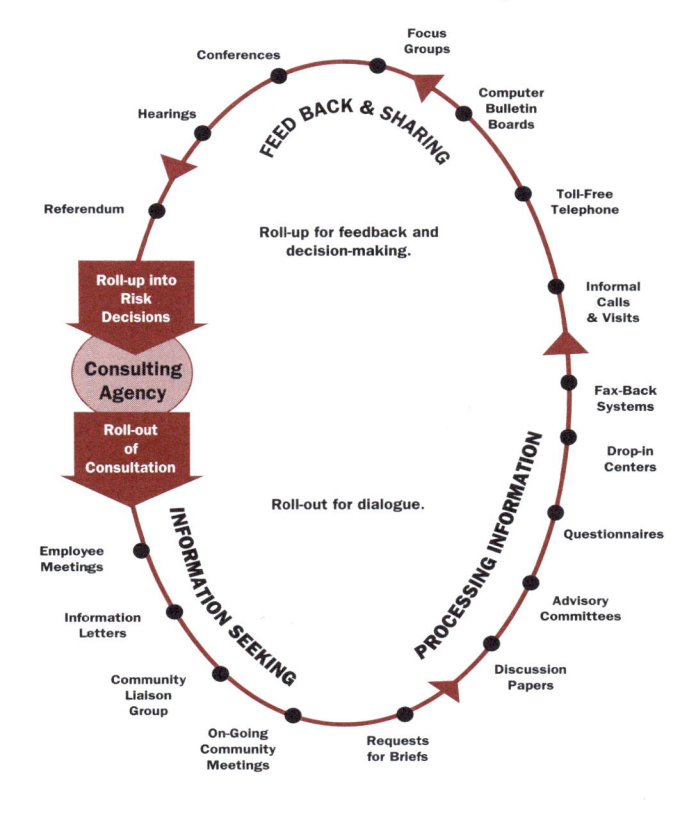

FEED BACK & SHARING

- Focus Groups
- Conferences
- Computer Bulletin Boards
- Hearings
- Toll-Free Telephone
- Referendum

Roll-up for feedback and decision-making.

Roll-up into Risk Decisions

Consulting Agency

Roll-out of Consultation

Roll-out for dialogue.

- Informal Calls & Visits
- Fax-Back Systems
- Drop-in Centers
- Questionnaires
- Advisory Committees
- Discussion Papers

PROCESSING INFORMATION

INFORMATION SEEKING

- Employee Meetings
- Information Letters
- Community Liaison Group
- On-Going Community Meetings
- Requests for Briefs

© 1996 McLoughlin MultiMedia Publishing Ltd.

Crisis Communications Plan

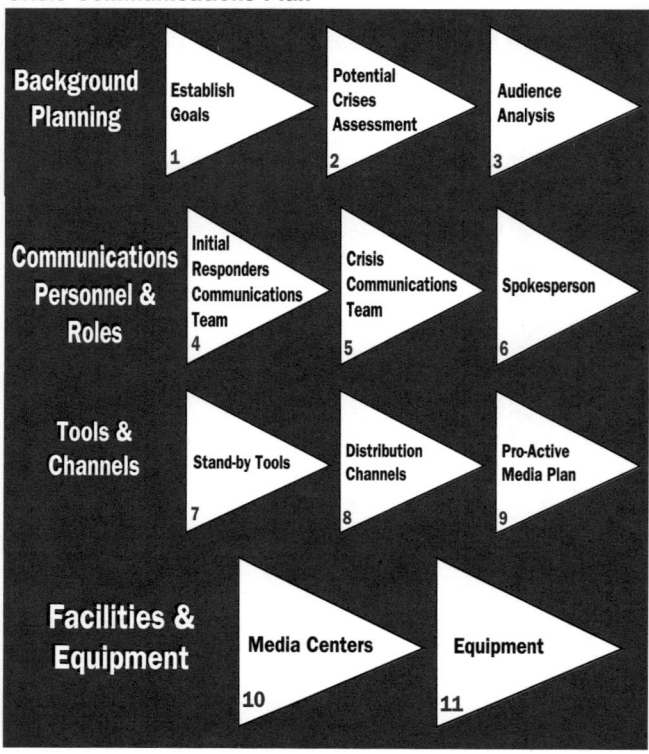

Background Planning
1. Establish Goals
2. Potential Crises Assessment
3. Audience Analysis

Communications Personnel & Roles
4. Initial Responders Communications Team
5. Crisis Communications Team
6. Spokesperson

Tools & Channels
7. Stand-by Tools
8. Distribution Channels
9. Pro-Active Media Plan

Facilities & Equipment
10. Media Centers
11. Equipment

© 1996 McLoughlin MultiMedia Publishing Ltd.

Crisis Communications Plan

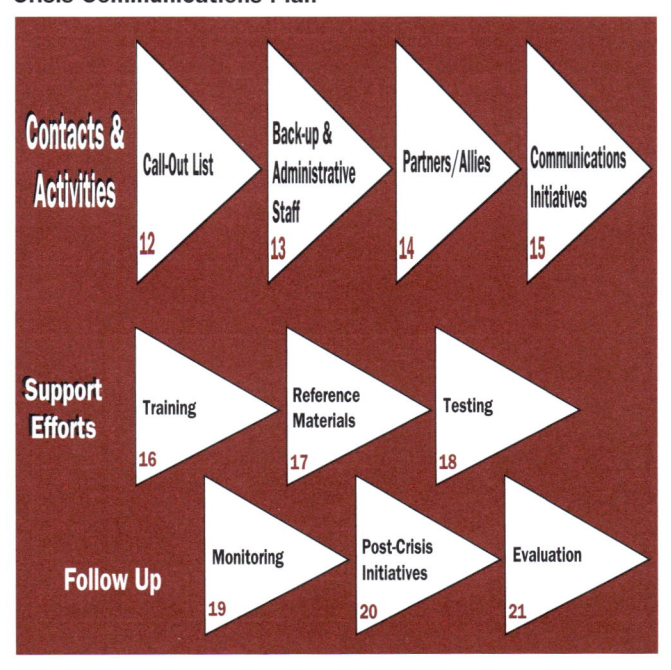

Contacts & Activities
- 12. Call-Out List
- 13. Back-up & Administrative Staff
- 14. Partners/Allies
- 15. Communications Initiatives

Support Efforts
- 16. Training
- 17. Reference Materials
- 18. Testing

Follow Up
- 19. Monitoring
- 20. Post-Crisis Initiatives
- 21. Evaluation

© 1996 McLoughlin MultiMedia Publishing Ltd.

Crisis Communications Team

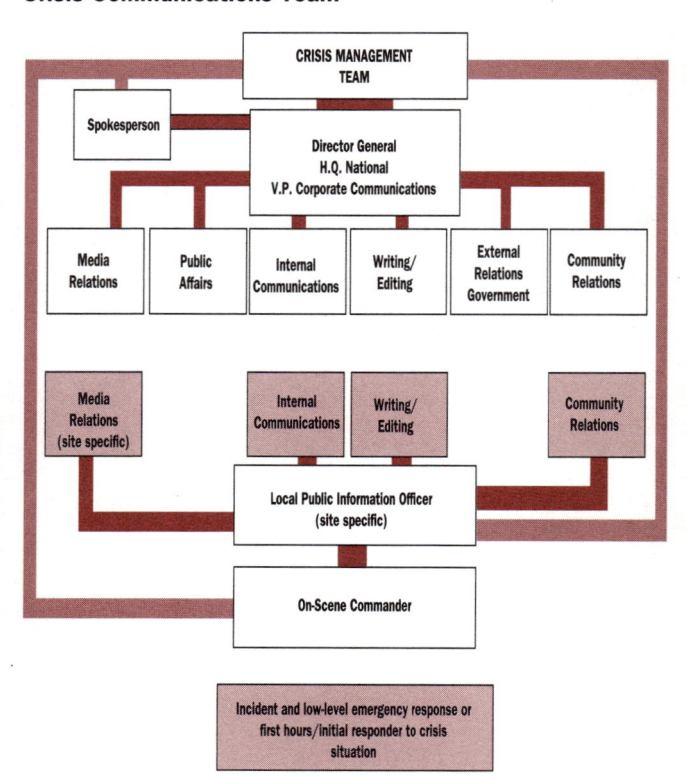

```
                    ┌─────────────────────┐
                    │ CRISIS MANAGEMENT   │
                    │       TEAM          │
                    └─────────────────────┘
    ┌──────────────┐          │
    │ Spokesperson │──┬───────┴──────────┐
    └──────────────┘  │  Director General │
                      │  H.Q. National    │
                      │ V.P. Corporate    │
                      │  Communications   │
                      └───────────────────┘
```

- Media Relations
- Public Affairs
- Internal Communications
- Writing/Editing
- External Relations Government
- Community Relations

- Media Relations (site specific)
- Internal Communications
- Writing/Editing
- Community Relations

Local Public Information Officer (site specific)

On-Scene Commander

Incident and low-level emergency response or first hours/initial responder to crisis situation

146 © 1996 McLoughlin MultiMedia Publishing Ltd.

Communicate With Power Risk Consultation Modeller™

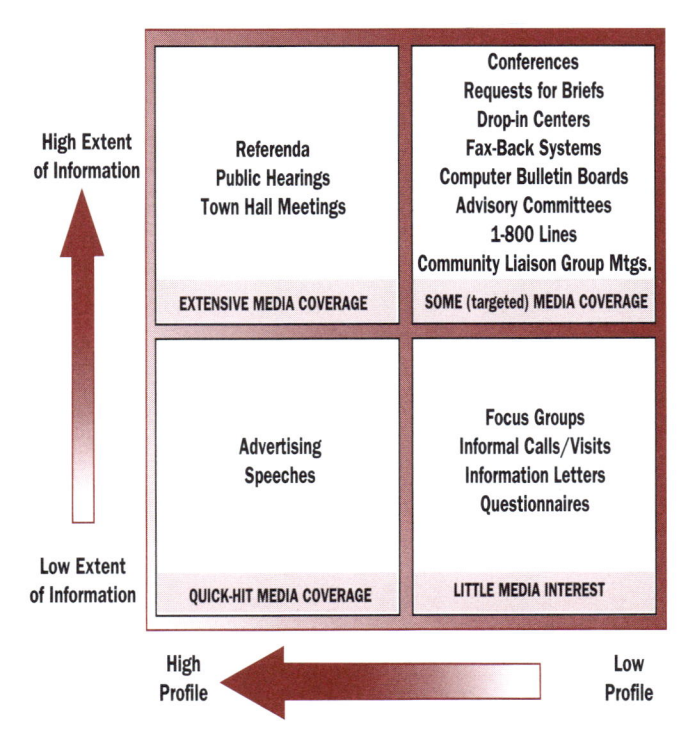

	High Profile	Low Profile
High Extent of Information	Referenda Public Hearings Town Hall Meetings EXTENSIVE MEDIA COVERAGE	Conferences Requests for Briefs Drop-in Centers Fax-Back Systems Computer Bulletin Boards Advisory Committees 1-800 Lines Community Liaison Group Mtgs. SOME (targeted) MEDIA COVERAGE
Low Extent of Information	Advertising Speeches QUICK-HIT MEDIA COVERAGE	Focus Groups Informal Calls/Visits Information Letters Questionnaires LITTLE MEDIA INTEREST

© 1996 McLoughlin MultiMedia Publishing Ltd.

Encountering the Media Issues Planner™

Encountering the Media Issues Planner™

1. Document Title
2. Issue Description
3. Media Analysis
4. Issue Analysis
5. Issue Management Goals
6. Strategy
7. Target Audiences
8. Stakeholders
9. Media Targets
10. Issue Management Team
11. Spokespersons
12. Messages, themes, etc.
13. Fact Gathering Requirements
14. Media Tools & Activities
15. Action Plan
16. Budget